COSMONAUTS
IN
ORBIT

GENE
AND
CLARE
GURNEY

COSMONAUTS IN ORBIT:

The Story of the Soviet Manned Space Program

FRANKLIN WATTS
New York, 1972

Cover design by Nick Krenitsky

All photographs are courtesy of the Information Department, Embassy of the Union of Soviet Socialist Republics. The illustrations on pp. 12, 41, 43, 44, 51, 83 and 150 are reproduced from *Review of the Soviet Space Program,* a Report of the Committee on Science and Astronautics, U.S. House of Representatives, 90th Congress.

Library of Congress Cataloging in Publication Data

Gurney, Gene.
    Cosmonauts in orbit.

    SUMMARY: Traces the development of Russia's space program and provides biographical material on the cosmonauts.

    1. Astronautics—Russia—Juvenile literature. 2. Astronauts—Russia—Juvenile literature. [1. Astronautics—Russia. 2. Astronauts—Russia] I. Gurney, Clare, joint author. II. Title.
TL789.8.R9G85   629.4'0947   76-189516
ISBN 0-531-02572-1

CONTENTS

1 | FIRST INTO SPACE: YURI GAGARIN AND VOSTOK 1 *7*

2 | THE RUSSIANS PREPARE THE WAY *22*

3 | A SECRET SOVIET SPACE PROGRAM *45*

4 | TWENTY-FIVE HOURS IN ORBIT — GHERMAN TITOV AND VOSTOK 2 *58*

5 | SPACE COMPANIONS *71*

6 | THE VOSKHOD REPLACES THE VOSTOK *92*

7 | FAILURE AND SUCCESS AT TYURATAM *111*

8 | SOYUZES IN ORBIT *124*

9 | UNMANNED EXPLORERS *147*

10 | AN ORBITING LABORATORY FOR THE COSMONAUTS *163*

INDEX *183*

1 | FIRST INTO SPACE: YURI GAGARIN AND VOSTOK 1

In Moscow it was ten o'clock on the morning of April 12, 1961, when an excited announcer interrupted a radio program with a special news bulletin. The bulletin came from Tass, the official Soviet news agency.

"Russia has successfully launched a man into space," the announcer reported. "His name is Yuri Gagarin. He was launched in a Sputnik named Vostok, which means east."

Tass had provided only a few details about the momentous first manned space flight, but these the announcer passed on to his listeners: The Sputnik weighed 10,395 pounds, or slightly over 5 tons. Its 89.1-minute journey around the earth had taken it to a maximum altitude of 302 kilometers (187¾ miles); its minimum altitude was 175 kilometers (109½ miles). Immediately after the launching Major Gagarin had reported that he was feeling well and that conditions in his cabin were normal. As he orbited the earth the spaceman was observed by radio telemetering devices and television.

After repeating the announcement two more times, the radio station resumed its normal program of music while Soviet citizens who had heard the stupendous news rushed to tell their friends. Rumors that a man would be launched into space had been circulating in Moscow for the past twenty-four hours. Now the launching was no longer an exciting rumor. It was a fact, confirmed by Tass and Radio Moscow.

Although only a few officials were aware of it, preparations for a manned space flight had been under way in the Soviet Union for many months. A group of pilots had been chosen and trained for the rigors of flight beyond the earth's atmosphere. A spacecraft had been developed for their use, and launching, tracking, and recovery systems had been worked out. When preparations were almost completed, one of the pilots, twenty-seven-year-old Yuri Gagarin, was selected as the first man to travel into space.

Yuri Alexeyevich Gagarin (the name Gagarin derives from the

First cosmonaut in space was Yuri Gagarin, pictured here fully suited up for space.

Russian word for wild duck) grew up in Klushino, a village about 100 miles west of Moscow in the Smolensk region of European Russia. He was a country boy whose father was a farmer and carpenter and whose mother was a milkmaid on a collective farm.

The pioneer spaceman saw his first airplanes during World War II when a pair of Russian air force fighters landed near his village. One of the planes had been damaged in battle, but its pilot was uninjured. The bemedaled flyers who climbed from the

1 | FIRST INTO SPACE

planes impressed Yuri and his friends. "We boys all wanted to be brave and handsome pilots," Yuri recalled later.

When he had completed six years of education, the future spaceman enrolled in a foundrymen's school in Moscow. Students at the school combined factory work and study while they prepared for jobs in Soviet industry. After one year, however, Yuri was accepted as a student at a four-year technical school where he could finish his secondary education while he also studied foundry work. His new school was in Saratov on the Volga River. Saratov also had a good flying school and an airfield.

Yuri Gagarin had never lost his desire to become a pilot. As soon as he was eligible, which was during his fourth year at Saratov, he enrolled at the flying school, where he studied the theory of flight and other aviation subjects at night. His course included a parachute jump, which he made from the wing of a training plane. After his successful jump, an instructor gave Yuri a ride in a Yak-18 fighter plane. "That first flight," he recalled, "filled me with pride and gave meaning to my whole life."

In the spring Yuri graduated with distinction as a foundryman-technician, and also received his ground school diploma from the flying school. He was determined to become a pilot. Instead of going to work as a foundryman, he spent the summer at an aviation camp, where he learned to fly the Yak-18. At the end of the summer he became an aviation cadet.

Yuri learned to fly jet planes at the Soviet Air Force's Orenburg Flying School. He was a good student, but, because he was short, he had difficulty lining up a plane for a landing. He solved this problem by sitting on a cushion. He graduated with honors in 1957, and shortly thereafter, as a newly commissioned lieutenant in the Soviet Air Force and as a new husband, recently married to a girl he had met in Orenburg, Gagarin volunteered for arctic flying duty.

The trailblazing Soviet earth satellites, Sputnik 1 and Sputnik 2, were launched in the fall of 1957. Sputnik 3 went into orbit on May 15, 1958. In 1959 the Soviet Union launched three Luna spacecraft. The first went into orbit around the sun; the second landed on the moon; and the third photographed the moon's far side. From his arctic station, Gagarin followed the progress of the Soviet space program. "I had an indefinite feeling that rockets were going to replace aircraft," he recalled later.

In the fall of 1959 Soviet Premier Nikita Khrushchev visited the United States. At the National Press Club in Washington, D.C., he was asked by a journalist: "When are you thinking of sending a man to the moon?"

Khrushchev answered: "We shall send a man to the moon when the necessary conditions have been created. So far the conditions do not exist."

When he read an account of the interview, Lieutenant Gagarin realized that serious preparation must be under way in the Soviet Union to send a man into space. Gagarin wanted to be that man. He decided to apply for space flight training.

Along with several dozen other candidates, all military pilots, Gagarin was called before a medical board. The candidates underwent a series of physical and psychological examinations. The tests were difficult. In one of the tests, Gagarin's ability to perform under adverse conditions was measured by having him work on math problems while a loudspeaker blared out possible answers. His eyes were examined seven times. "The board was stricter than anything I had ever known before," he said afterward.

Gagarin was among the 10 percent who survived the first elimination, but he had to face a second medical board for more tests. "The doctors this time were doubly exacting," Gagarin recalled. He was tested in a pressure chamber and in a centrifuge. His memory, reaction time, the speed with which his attention could be shifted from one thing to another, and his ability to perform precise movements were all measured. He also answered questions about his family, friends, social life, and cultural interests.

When the final reviewing doctor told him: "The stratosphere is not the limit for you," Yuri knew he had passed the tests successfully. He left the Arctic soon after his twenty-sixth birthday for a new base where he began the training that culminated in the flight of Vostok 1.

Yuri Gagarin's big day began at dawn at the Soviet cosmodrome near Tyuratam, just east of the Aral Sea. (The cosmodrome is sometimes called Baikonur, although it is located closer to Tyuratam than to Baikonur.) With his substitute, Gherman Titov, he had spent the night in a small brown cottage with interior walls of robin's-egg blue. The cosmonauts were awakened by their doctor. (The Soviets chose the designation cosmonaut, derived from the Greek word *kosmos,* meaning "world," or "universe," for their spacemen. The American term astronaut derives from the Greek *astron,* meaning "star.") After setting-up exercises, Gagarin and Titov ate a breakfast of chopped meat, blackberry jam, and coffee. The breakfast, like all of their meals for the past several days, was eaten from tubes because the food carried by the Vostok would be packaged in tubes.

There was a brief medical examination before Gagarin and Titov began the complicated process of dressing for space flight. If anything happened to disqualify Yuri Gagarin before the launching of the Vostok, his substitute had to be ready to take over at once. Therefore, technicians prepared both men for the trip into space.

Medical sensors that would tell doctors on the ground how the man in space was faring were taped to the cosmonauts' bodies. Over these went sky-blue thermal underwear and bright orange space suits. The suits were tested for pressure seal and their instruments and connections were checked. The cosmonauts' parachute instructor had some last-minute advice on leaving the spacecraft and the man who had designed the Vostok arrived to give them final instructions.

At last Gagarin and Titov were ready to leave their quarters. As they walked to a waiting bus, the two men made a vivid picture in their orange space suits and white airtight helmets with CCCP in large letters on the front. (In the Russian language, the Union of Soviet Socialist Republics is Soyuz Sovetskikh Sotsialisticheskikh Respublic and in the Russian alphabet the initials for these words are C.C.C.P.) Under the helmets they wore inner helmets equipped with earphones.

It was an almost cloudless April day, ideal weather for a launching. The blue and white bus took the cosmonauts to the Tyuratam launching pad, where a tall silver-hulled rocket gleamed in the early morning sunshine. At its tip rested the spaceship Vostok. Gagarin was to write later that the Vostok was "beautiful, more beautiful than a locomotive, steamship, plane, palaces and bridges, all put together. I beheld not only a remarkable piece of machinery, but also an impressive work of art." He had only a moment to admire the spaceship, however. Government officials and technicians were waiting at the launching pad to see him off. The cosmonaut saluted the chairman of the State Commission for the First Space Flight. "Senior Lieutenant Gagarin is ready for the first flight in the spaceship Vostok," he announced.

The chairman replied by wishing Gagarin luck and a happy landing and the cosmonaut moved toward the service-tower elevator that would carry him up to the Vostok. Before entering the elevator he paused to make a statement for the press and radio. "Dear friends, both known and unknown to me, fellow country-

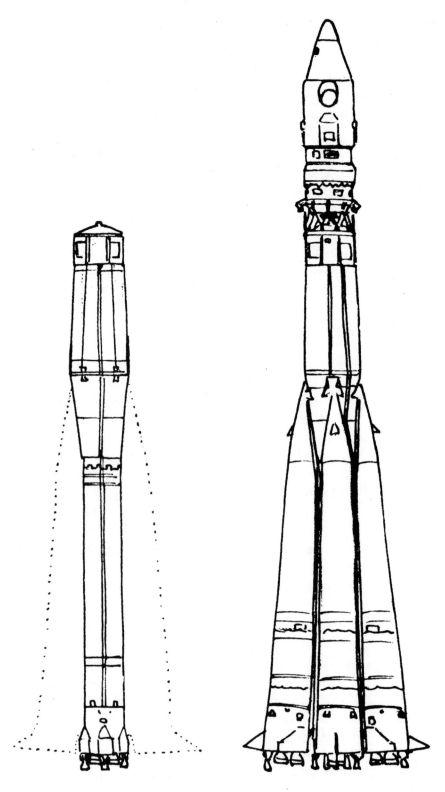

Sketch of the standard Soviet launch vehicle Vostok, showing central core and total assembly with four strap-ons.

men, men and women of all lands and continents," he began. "In a few minutes a mighty spaceship will take me into the far-away expanses of the universe. What can I say to you in these last minutes before the start? I see my whole past life as one wonderful moment. Everything I have experienced and done till now has been in preparation for this moment. You must realize that it is hard to express my feeling now that the test for which we have been training ardently and long is at hand. I don't have to tell you what I felt when it was suggested that I should make this flight, the first in history. Was it joy? No, it was something more than that. Pride? No, it was not just pride. I felt very happy — to be the first in space, to engage in an unprecedented duel with nature — could anyone dream of anything greater than that?"

After commenting on the tremendous responsibility of being the first man to travel in space and his determination to make his mission a success, Cosmonaut Gagarin took leave of his earth-bound audience. "It is a matter of minutes now before the start," he observed. "I say to you, good-bye, dear friends, just as people say to each other when setting out on a long journey. I would like very much to embrace you all, people known and unknown to me, close friends and strangers alike."

With a cheerful "See you soon!" the orange-suited spaceman stepped into the elevator for the fifteen-story ride to the top of the rocket. Watchers on the ground saw him move from the elevator to the Vostok and they saw the hatch door close after he entered the spacecraft.

In the nearby control center where the countdown for the launching of Vostok 1 was in progress, red, amber, and green lights glowed on the consoles. Several television screens showed Gagarin securely strapped in his seat. He was checking the spacecraft's equipment. "Hello, Earth, I am Cosmonaut," he radioed to the control center. "I have tested the communications. The tumblers on the control panel are in the assigned initial position. The globe is at the point of division. Pressure in the cabin, unity; humidity, 65 percent; temperature, 19 degrees centigrade; pressure in the compartment, 1.2 [atmospheres]; pressure in the orientation system, normal. I feel fine and am ready for the start."

From the control center the technical flight supervisor announced that one hour remained before lift-off, then, later, thirty minutes. The cosmonaut was informed that his face could be seen clearly on the television screens. He replied: "My heart beats normally. I feel fine. I have put on the gloves, closed the helmet, and am ready for the start."

1 | FIRST INTO SPACE

At 9:07 A.M., Moscow time, the countdown ended. When he heard the lift-off command, the cosmonaut radioed: "Off we go. Everything is normal."

With a burst of flame and a mighty roar, the rocket beneath the Vostok rose from the launching pad. Inside the spacecraft Gagarin heard what he described as a "shrill whistle and a mounting roar." But the noise was no greater than that heard inside the cabin of a jet aircraft.

The cosmonaut's couch-like seat in the Vostok had been especially designed to minimize the stresses of launching when the rapid climb of the rocket would expose the spaceman to high gravity, or g, forces. The seat could not completely counteract the increasing g-forces, however. Seventy seconds after lift-off, Gagarin was radioing: "I feel well. Am continuing flight. The g-forces are increasing. Everything is all right." He recalled later that he could hardly move his hands and feet and he felt as though an "uncompromising force" was riveting him to his seat.

At this stage of his journey the cosmonaut could not see outside his spacecraft. The Vostok was still covered by a shroud to protect it from atmospheric friction. Once the thickest portion of the atmosphere had been left behind, however, the protective shroud was automatically jettisoned. "How magnificent!" Gagarin exclaimed at his first sight of the earth. He was above a broad Siberian river dotted with sunlit islands. When the Vostok went into orbit around the earth, the rocket that had lifted it high into space was jettisoned also.

In orbit now, Gagarin was weightless, the first man to experience that sensation for more than a few seconds at a time. After his pioneer flight, the cosmonaut told a Soviet journalist: "When weightlessness came I felt fine. Everything was easier to do. And this stands to reason. My legs and arms did not weigh anything. The objects floated in the cabin. Nor did I keep my seat as I had until then, but was suspended in the air. During the state of weightlessness I ate and drank, everything went on as it does on earth. I even worked in this state; I wrote down my observations. My handwriting was the same, although my hand did not weigh anything. I had to hold on to the notepad, though, or it would have floated away. I maintained radio communication in different channels and used a telegraph key. I saw that weightlessness does not in any way affect one's capacity for work."

As Vostok 1 traveled around the earth at nearly 18,000 miles an hour, the cosmonaut was fascinated by what he saw inside and outside his spacecraft. He radioed his observations to earth or recorded them in his notebook or on tape. He watched some drops of liquid that had escaped from a tube take on a spherical shape and float about in the cabin until they made contact with the glass in a porthole. The spaceman reported that they clung to the glass "like dew to a flower."

Gagarin found the sun to be remarkably bright. From time to time he had to cover the Vostok's portholes with special filters. He did not see the moon because it was never in his field of vision, but the stars were dazzling against the blackness of space.

Below the Vostok, the earth presented an ever-changing panorama. Gagarin reported that water looked "darkish, with faintly gleaming spots." He could make out continental coastlines, islands, large rivers, and mountains. And he observed that the earth was indeed round. "On the horizon," he noted, "I could see the sharp contrasting change from the light surface of the earth to the inky blackness of the sky. The earth was gay with a lavish palette of colors. It had a pale blue halo around it. Then this band gradually darkened, became turquoise, blue, violet, and then coal black. This change is very beautiful and pleasing to the eye."

When the Vostok passed into the earth's shadow, a somewhat surprised cosmonaut noted: "It suddenly became pitch dark."

At 9:52 A.M., Moscow time, Vostok 1 was over South America. "The flight is proceeding normally. I feel well. The on-board apparatus is working faultlessly," the cosmonaut radioed. He reported that he was eating and drinking at the scheduled times, although he was neither hungry nor thirsty.

From high over Africa at 10:15 A.M. the cosmonaut sent the reassuring message: "Flight proceeding normally, am feeling no ill effects from weightlessness."

Vostok 1 was equipped with an automatic orientation system that aligned the spacecraft with the sun. If the automatic guidance system had failed, the cosmonaut could have controlled the craft himself, but this was not necessary. The automatic system also kept the Vostok's retro-, or braking, rockets facing the planned direction of flight. Gagarin was depending on the retro-rockets to slow down the spacecraft sufficiently at the end of its journey for the force of gravity to pull it back toward earth.

At 10:25, one hour and eighteen minutes after lift-off, the all-important braking rockets fired automatically, precisely as planned. The hurtling Vostok slowed and began to lose altitude. Inside the craft, the cosmonaut braced himself for the most dangerous part of his pioneering space mission.

Gagarin knew that the external skin of the Vostok would become red hot as the spaceship passed through the thickening atmosphere. He also knew that the Vostok had been constructed to withstand the terrific heat. Nevertheless, he became somewhat apprehensive as he plummeted toward the earth. "Through the porthole filters I saw the frightening crimson reflection of the flames raging all around the ship," he said later. Inside the cabin, however, the temperature remained at a reassuring 20 degrees centigrade.

The cosmonaut had other causes for anxiety. "The ship began to rotate," he recalled, "and I reported this to earth. But the rotation, which worried me, quickly stopped and the further descent proceeded normally." And he described the g-forces during descent as "much greater than the stresses I had experienced on takeoff."

At a predetermined altitude, huge drogue parachutes opened to slow the Vostok's plunge. Later Vostok cosmonauts were to eject from the falling spacecraft and finish the landing under their own parachutes, but Gagarin was still inside the ship's cabin when it touched down in a plowed field of the Leninsky Put (Lenin's Path) collective farm near the town of Engels. The pioneer spaceman had been aloft for one hour and forty-eight minutes and in orbit around the earth for one hour and twenty-nine minutes.

Because the landing was a few miles from the airfield that had been selected as the target area, there was no official party to greet the returned cosmonaut. His landing was not unobserved, however. A woman and a girl saw the descending Vostok and rushed to the field. When the orange-clad cosmonaut emerged from the spacecraft, they viewed him with some alarm. "Did you come from outer space?" the woman asked.

"Just imagine it! I certainly have!" a smiling Gagarin answered.

A group of tractor operators also saw the Vostok land. They came rushing across the fields shouting the cosmonaut's name. The tractor operators were followed by some soldiers, who addressed him as Major Gagarin. The spaceman had been promoted in flight.

Before he left the landing site, Gagarin examined the craft that had carried him around the earth. He was pleased with what he found. "The ship and the equipment in it were in good enough condition to be used for another space flight," he said later.

Yuri Gagarin had begun his journey into space as a trained and skillful, but unknown, cosmonaut. He returned to earth a national hero. Shortly after landing, he received a congratulatory

Yuri Gagarin receives a hero's welcome at Vnukovo Airport after the completion of the first space flight in April, 1961.

telegram from Soviet Premier Nikita Khrushchev and he spoke with the premier on the telephone. During the conversation, the cosmonaut assured Khrushchev that he had felt quite at home in his spaceship and that the ship's equipment had worked well.

Ordinary Soviet citizens were anxious to greet the returned spaceman too. Their opportunity came at a huge celebration held in Moscow's Red Square on April 14. Only one day, the 13th, had been set aside for the cosmonaut's postflight physical examination, debriefing, and rest. Gagarin flew to Moscow in an Ilyushin-18 jet that was escorted by seven MIG fighters. At Vnukovo Airport thousands of excited Russians cheered his arrival. Government leaders crowded a flower-bedecked rostrum about 50 yards from the Ilyushin. A bright red carpet extended from the plane to the rostrum.

Later, the cosmonaut was to write of his seemingly endless walk down that red carpet: "I had to go, and go alone, and I went.

　　　　　　　　　　　　　　　1 | FIRST INTO SPACE

I never felt so nervous in all my life, not even when I was up there in the spaceship. That stretch of carpet was long, very long. And while I walked along it, I was able to recover from my astonishment and collect myself.

"I walked on with television and all sorts of other cameras trained on me. All of a sudden I felt that one of my shoe laces had come undone. What if I should tread on it and stretch out on the red carpet right in front of all the people? There certainly would be a laugh then and some embarrassment, too. Out in space I didn't fall, but here on the ground I had lost my footing!"

The cosmonaut reached the rostrum safely, however. He officially reported that he had successfully fulfilled his assignment and received the congratulations of the assembled dignitaries. Then he entered an open car to head a motorcade to Red Square.

Since early morning, Soviet citizens had been lining the streets leading to Red Square. The square itself was filled with people, many of whom carried banners and pictures of the cosmonaut. From a reviewing stand in the square, Gagarin spoke to the crowd. He expressed his gratitude for the opportunity to make the first flight into space and said that he had had no doubt whatsoever that the flight would be successful. Soviet spaceships, he predicted, would one day fly even more distant routes.

During the Red Square ceremonies, the pioneer spaceman was awarded the title Hero of the Soviet Union, his country's highest honor. His accomplishment was indeed a great one. He had ventured where no man had gone before and faced hazards that were unknown, or at best, known only through simulation on earth.

The g-forces that Gagarin had experienced during launching and landing might easily have been much greater than anticipated, or he could have reacted unfavorably to prolonged weightlessness. Vostok 1 might have been unable to withstand the hostile space environment or the intense heat of reentry into the earth's atmosphere. Moreover, there was the danger of a possible collision with a meteoroid in space. And no one knew for sure how a man would react psychologically to the remoteness of space flight.

Yuri Gagarin's pioneering journey proved that man could function in space. Soviet pronouncements hailed the "unequaled victory of man over the forces of nature." Academician A. N. Nesmeyanov, the president of the Soviet Academy of Sciences, said in an interview: "The flight of Yuri Gagarin has ushered in a new era, not only in the development of science, but in the history of all mankind. The road to the planets is open."

Citizens line the streets of Moscow, waiting for a glimpse of Cosmonaut Gagarin after his successful flight.

Gagarin's feat was acclaimed in other countries as well. Sir Bernard Lovell, a leading British scientist, called the flight one of the greatest scientific achievements in history. French scientists praised it as a prodigious scientific, technical, and human exploit. In Italy, where banner headlines heralded the flight, the newspaper *L'Osservatore romano* said: "This first successful space launching of man fixes a memorable moment in scientific history and progress."

Indian Prime Minister Jawaharlal Nehru hailed the orbiting of the earth as "a great human victory of man over the forces of nature." In Peking, China, residents were said to have beaten drums and gongs to celebrate the happy event.

John F. Kennedy, the President of the United States, congratulated the Soviet Union on its "outstanding technical accomplishment"; and James E. Webb, head of the National Aeronautics and Space Administration, described the first manned space flight as "a significant accomplishment that demonstrates great technical capacity."

Countless other Americans praised the Soviet Union's achievement. They were sincere in their commendations, but there was disappointment, too, because many Americans had hoped that the United States would be the first country to launch a man into space.

On April 12, when Vostok 1 made its pioneering journey into earth orbit, a Redstone rocket stood on a launching pad at Cape Canaveral, Florida (since renamed Cape Kennedy), where the United States was completing preparations for its first manned space flight. It was not to be an orbital flight, however. Instead, the Redstone rocket was to boost a capsule containing Astronaut Alan B. Shepard, Jr., more than 100 miles up into space. The capsule would then return to earth. This was to be a test flight for the United States Project Mercury, which would eventually put astronauts into orbit around the earth.

Project Mercury had already launched unmanned capsules into space to test them. Two Mercury capsules had carried monkeys and another capsule had had a chimpanzee as a passenger. The animals all returned to earth safely.

Prior to the Project Mercury tests, the United States had launched a variety of instrument-carrying rockets that obtained scientific data from altitudes high above the earth without going into orbit. Explorer 1, the first United States earth satellite, was launched on January 31, 1958, some four months after the Soviet

Union launched Sputnik 1 and three months after the launching of Sputnik 2. Explorer 1 weighed a mere 31 pounds, compared with the 184 pounds of Sputnik 1 and the 1,121 pounds of Sputnik 2.

During 1958 the United States also launched a small Vanguard satellite that obtained information about the size and shape of the earth and another Explorer that continued Explorer 1's study of radiation in space. And at the end of the year, a Project Score satellite was broadcasting a recorded message from President Dwight D. Eisenhower as it traveled around the earth.

In 1959 the United States sent a Discoverer satellite into polar orbit and a Pioneer satellite into orbit around the sun. Another United States satellite took the first crude television pictures of the earth.

During 1960, a second United States satellite went into solar orbit, and the first weather and navigational satellites were launched.

But the United States had not been able to send an unmanned spaceship to the moon as the Soviet Union had done with its Lunas. And its first manned space flight did not leave Cape Canaveral until three weeks after Cosmonaut Yuri Gagarin had orbited the earth in Vostok 1.

1 | FIRST INTO SPACE

2 | THE RUSSIANS PREPARE THE WAY

Yuri Gagarin's successful space flight surprised a great many people who did not think the Soviet Union was technically capable of such an achievement. But the flight was not a lucky accident. It was based on many years of study and experimentation in aviation and rocketry by Russian scientists and inventors.

Experiments with flying machines may have begun in Russia as early as 1754 when Mikhail Lomonosov, a poet and scientist, is said to have constructed a working model of a helicopter, which he called an aerodromic machine. The model, powered by a watch spring, consisted of two pairs of wings that lifted a small box containing thermometers and other meteorological instruments. Lomonosov's aerodromic machine never rose very high, even after he strengthened its spring and increased the distance between its wings.

The Russians claim that a scribe named Kriakutnoy built and navigated a balloon in 1731, fifty-two years before the Montgolfier brothers developed their glôbe aerostatique. There is no evidence of the scribe's flight, however. The first successful Russian balloon flight of which there is a record took place in 1804 at St. Petersburg (now Leningrad). The pilot was an Englishman, but a Russian supervised the balloon's inflation. During the nineteenth century, several Russians experimented with balloon design in an attempt to improve lift and control. Among them was the noted chemist Dmitri Mendeléyev, who, in 1888, ascended to 16,000 feet in a stratostat of his own design to observe an eclipse of the sun.

While some nineteenth-century Russians were experimenting with balloons, others were working with ideas for heavier-than-air craft. The Russians claim that Alexander Mozhaisky, a young naval officer, actually invented the first airplane. Inspired by the flight of birds, he built model airplanes and successfully demonstrated them in 1876. The models were said to be much more advanced than any other models developed in Europe at that time. Mozhaisky submitted blueprints to the Chief Engineering Office in St.

22

Petersburg in 1877 and received a patent for his invention. In 1882 his plane was ready to be flown; according to some accounts, it did fly. But there is no record of such a flight and no blueprints have ever been found.

Drawings do exist, however, for the electroplane that Alexander Lodyghin designed in 1869. It was a helicopter with two airscrews (propellers), one to lift the machine and the other to direct its flight. Two other nineteenth-century Russians, M. A. Ryhachev and Y. S. Fyodorov, made pioneer studies of the use of airscrews in flying machines.

By 1880 a group of Russians who were interested in the problems of flight had organized the Society for Air Navigation. *Vozdukhoplavated (The Air Navigator)*, Russia's first aviation magazine, began publication that same year.

Nikolai Zhukovsky, one of Russia's leading aerodynamicists, became interested in flying during the 1880's following his study of motion stability and hydromechanics (the branch of physics that deals with the equilibrium and motion of fluids and their effects on solids). Between 1890 and 1900 he published forty-four papers on the theory of flight and the laws of motion. In 1898 Zhukovsky predicted that heavier-than-air craft would provide the means for one or two people to fly rapidly in the desired direction. Such craft "would make us cease envying the birds," Zhukovsky said. He also predicted that man's intellect, rather than the strength of his muscles, would make it possible for him to fly.

Igor Sikorsky, another of Russia's aviation pioneers, became interested in helicopters when his mother showed him a picture of the sixteenth-century Italian painter Leonardo da Vinci's helicopter. Sikorsky's first attempt at helicopter design resulted in a model propelled by rubber bands. As a student at the Kiev Polytechnic Institute, the mechanically inclined youth built a steam-powered motorcycle, but his real interest was in helicopters, which he believed were more practical than fixed-wing planes. Sikorsky's first machine was a failure because he lacked a suitable engine. Although he tried again, he eventually turned to fixed-wing craft and produced several four-engine planes that were notable for their large size and long range. During World War I, Sikorsky built multi-engine bombers for Russia and for France. After the war he moved to the United States, where he became a successful aircraft manufacturer. In 1939 he returned to the development of helicopters.

In the Soviet Union, meanwhile, the Zhukovsky Central Aero-

Igor Sikorsky, the Russian aviation pioneer who later came to the United States to design and build helicopters.

Hydrodynamic Institute in Moscow took the lead in aviation research and training. Soviet aviators in Russian-built planes made several spectacular flights. Among them was the July, 1937, non-stop flight of a four-engine ANT-25 bomber from Moscow to San Jacinto, California, by way of the North Pole.

During World War II, the Soviet Union produced a very good fighter plane called the Sturmovik. After the war, however, the Russians relied largely on DC-3 planes, which they had acquired from the United States and copied, while they developed jet-propelled planes for civilian and military use. The Soviet Union was the first country to introduce jet planes for civilian transportation.

The Russians were interested in rockets long before they became a source of power for flight. The earliest known writing by a Russian on the subject was by Onisim Mikhailov, a master of gunnery, in 1607. He described combat rockets as "cannonballs that run and fly."

The first rockets were fired in Russia late in the seventeenth century. They were Chinese rockets imported by Czar Peter I. Peter moved a rocket works, originally established in Moscow in 1680, to St. Petersburg and enlarged it. He was interested in rockets for fireworks as well as for his soldiers to use.

Russian fireworks were world-famous during Peter's reign and later. In Russia there were lavish displays of fireworks at feasts, festivals, and other celebrations. The Russians developed a variety of pyrotechnic mixtures and several thousand workers were employed in rocket and powder production.

Alexander Zasiadko, a Russian artillery officer, designed what he called a fighting rocket in 1815. The rocket was essentially a length of pipe open at one end with a wooden tail to help maintain the direction of flight. The charge was a mixture of gunpowder and charcoal. When the charge was set afire, gases rushed out the open end of the pipe and the recoil pushed the rocket up. In 1826 Zasiadko formed Russia's first military rocket company. He later invented a special launching stand for rockets.

Russia employed rockets in combat for the first time during its conflict with Turkey in 1828–29. Soldiers assembled thousands of rockets near the front lines because of the difficulty of transporting them. Rockets designed by William Congreve, a British army officer, had already been used as weapons in Europe and in the United States, where the British employed them at Bladensburg and Fort McHenry during the War of 1812. It was the rocket attack on Fort McHenry that inspired Francis Scott Key to write

"The Star-Spangled Banner," which was set to music and later adopted as the United States national anthem.

Konstantin Konstantinov, a military engineer who lived from 1818 to 1871, was one of the first of many Russians who were to suggest that rockets might be used as a vehicle of travel. The Russians consider Konstantinov to be the founder of experimental rocketry. He developed a ballistic pendulum to measure the reaction force of rockets, and he made a pioneer study of the relationship between a rocket's form and structure and its flight path.

Two contemporaries of Konstantinov proposed that rockets be used to propel passenger-carrying balloons. I. I. Tretesky suggested that gunpowder, steam, gas, or compressed air might be used as rocket fuel. Nicholas Sokovin's plan involved a rocket-powered balloon shaped like a turtle that moved when compressed air was forced into its bag. The Russians later claimed that Sokovin had a jet-propelled dirigible in mind.

A young Russian explosives maker named Nicholas Kibalchich became convinced that heavier-than-air craft could be powered by rockets. While he was in prison charged with preparing the explosives for the bombs that killed Czar Alexander II, Kibalchich drew sketches of a rocket plane powered by successive explosions of compressed-powder candles. He was unable to do any further work on his idea, however, because he was found guilty and hanged in 1881.

Another of Russia's rocket pioneers was the engineer and architect Fydor R. Geshvend. His observations of wild geese in flight led him to believe that with the aid of rockets man, too, could fly. He designed a jet propulsion engine, which he rated at "350 goosepower," and a rocket with several low-end openings, a design that the Soviets now claim Geshvend was the first to utilize. They also credit Geshvend with working out a way to use jet power for a plane's vertical takeoff and landing.

Not content with writing about his ideas and making sketches of them, Geshvend rented land near Kiev and prepared to launch rockets from a platform equipped with rails. His experiments failed, however, and their cost bankrupted him. He died in 1890 at the age of forty-nine.

Some of the fundamentals of the theory of rocket propulsion were developed in Russia in the years between 1897 and 1904 by Ivan Meshchersky, a professor at the St. Petersburg Polytechnic Institute. His equations of the motions of bodies with variable mass have been credited with making the Sputniks possible.

Greatest of all Russian rocket pioneers was Konstantin Tsiolkovsky.

The Soviet Union esteems all of its rocket pioneers, but the greatest honor goes to Konstantin Eduardovitch Tsiolkovsky, a self-taught scientist who worked out important principles of rocket propulsion and designed space vehicles as well.

Tsiolkovsky was born in 1857 in the village of Izhevskoye. His father was a poorly paid forester and an unsuccessful inventor. Konstantin was apparently a precocious child who liked science and mathematics. At eight, when he received a small hydrogen-filled balloon from his mother, he became interested in investigating the effects of gravity. Unfortunately, a severe case of scarlet

2 | THE RUSSIANS PREPARE THE WAY

fever the next year left him almost totally deaf. Because he could not hear his teachers, he had to leave school and continue his education by studying at home.

When Konstantin wasn't busy with his books, he made a variety of machines. He built a small turner's lathe and used it to construct a tiny turbine-powered carriage. Remembering the balloon he had received from his mother, he made one of tissue paper and filled it with enough smoke to enable it to float. He also built aircraft models with flapping wings and experimented with an astrolabe and a homemade range finder.

At sixteen Konstantin went to Moscow to continue his education in the libraries there. He had very little money to spend on food and lodging. In his autobiography he wrote of those days: "I remember very well that I had nothing to eat but dark bread and water. I would go to a bakery once in three days and buy nine kopeks' worth of bread. . . . For all that, I was happy with my ideas, and my diet of dark bread did not dampen my spirits."

Out of his small allowance, Konstantin managed to buy chemicals and apparatus for experiments that he conducted in his room. With the help of an ear trumpet, which he made himself, he was able to enjoy Moscow's free scientific lectures. All scientific subjects interested the young man, but his thoughts began to turn more and more to the possibilities of space travel.

For a short time Konstantin believed that he had solved the problem of launching an object into space. He reasoned that centrifugal force, the force that causes an object to move away from a center of rotation, could be incorporated in a launching device. He built a box holding two pendulums, each topped with a ball that traveled in an arc as its pendulum swung. If his theory was correct, centrifugal force would cause the box to move upward indefinitely. But the box didn't move at all, and Konstantin realized that he had failed to understand how centrifugal force worked.

When he was nineteen, Konstantin Tsiolkovsky left Moscow and rejoined his family. He became a tutor and, after passing an examination, a teacher of arithmetic, geometry, and physics.

Tsiolkovsky enjoyed teaching, but he enjoyed his scientific experiments with electricity and gases even more. From his experiments he learned that particles of gas moved in straight lines at a high velocity until they encountered one another. Then they changed direction and velocity. The pressure of gas, he concluded, was due to the impact of particles against the walls of a container.

This is the kinetic theory of gases and it had already been discovered, although Tsiolkovsky did not know it. He wrote a paper describing his ideas about gases and sent it to the Society of Physics and Chemistry in St. Petersburg. The officers of the society realized that Tsiolkovsky, who lived in a small, isolated village that lacked learned societies and scientific publications, had no way of keeping up with developments in physics. They praised him for the way he had conducted his study of gases and encouraged him to continue his scientific investigations.

Occasionally the young scientist used his knowledge to amuse himself and the residents of his village. He constructed a bird that resembled a vulture and, choosing a day when the air currents were right, set the bird to soaring above the town on its large, kitelike wings. He also equipped an armchair with sled runners and a sail. In this contrivance he sped over a frozen river in the wintertime.

Most of Tsiolkovsky's free time was devoted to serious studies. He later wrote: "The chief goal of my life was not to waste my years but to help mankind in its progress, even if only a little. What interested me gave me neither bread nor influence, but I hoped, and still hope, that my work will, perhaps soon, perhaps in the far-off future, give society mountains of bread and an incalculable amount of power."

Konstantin Tsiolkovsky continued to be intrigued by the possibility of space travel. He was unable to work out a method of launching an object into space, but he investigated the properties of the atmosphere, speculated on the nature of space, and designed a craft for interplanetary travel.

The self-taught scientist used some of his ideas about space travel in the science-fiction stories that he began to write in 1887. One story was entitled "On the Moon." Others were "Daydreaming of Sky and Earth" and "Outside the Earth." He also wrote fairy tales and poems based on the idea of space travel.

In 1886 Tsiolkovsky wrote an essay describing his plan for an all-metal dirigible. He included blueprints showing just how such a dirigible should be constructed. Tsiolkovsky's dirigible was never more than a set of blueprints, but the Russians say that if it had been built, it would have been the first lighter-than-air craft to have a lifting power unaffected by varying temperatures and altitudes. To accomplish this, Tsiolkovsky had worked out a corrugated skin for his dirigible and a method of altering its volume. The metal of the skin was to have been treated for durability by a special process developed by the inventor. He also planned to use engine exhaust to warm the hydrogen that filled the airship.

The shape that Tsiolkovsky developed for his dirigible and his use of a thin, but strong, metal skin have been praised by aeronautical engineers, especially those in the Soviet Union. But critics point out that Tsiolkovsky's method of heating gas for his dirigible would not have worked. In any case, an unsympathetic government denied the inventor's request for funds to construct a working model of the dirigible. He did gain some recognition, however. In 1887 he was invited to Moscow to speak on his aerostat (the Russians used this term for both balloons and dirigibles) before a scientific society, whose members praised the ideas of the inventive schoolteacher.

Tsiolkovsky continued to work on dirigible designs and on a design for a heavier-than-air craft as well. What he had in mind in the latter case was a streamlined, single-winged plane of metal. He described it in an article entitled "Airplane, or Bird-like (Aviational), Flying Machine." The article included drawings of the plane. Tsiolkovsky did not try to duplicate the flapping wings of a bird, but concentrated instead on the aerodynamic principles that govern a bird's soaring.

Later Russian writers were to insist that Tsiolkovsky's plane, designed in 1894, was superior to the one the Wright brothers flew at Kitty Hawk in 1903. They especially praised Tsiolkovsky's use of a streamlined shape and the aerodynamically advanced design of the wings. Yet Tsiolkovsky's plane was never built; therefore, it is impossible to compare it with the plane actually flown by the Wrights.

Tsiolkovsky went on to construct a wind tunnel, which enabled him to study the aerodynamic characteristics of different shapes. His attention turned more and more to rocket propulsion, however. As early as 1883 he had suggested that "reactive movement" was a possible power source for flying machines. Now he began to consider rockets in connection with space travel. In his first paper on the subject, finished in 1903, he discussed the use of rockets to explore the upper reaches of the atmosphere and possibly the planets. He also suggested that man-made satellites could be launched to orbit the earth.

In the following years, Tsiolkovsky continued to develop his ideas about rockets. By 1929 he had worked out the details of two multistage rockets. One, which he called a rocket-train, consisted of a series of rockets fastened together with the least powerful at the bottom. As the rockets exhausted their fuel, they dropped off until only one remained at the rocket's destination. This is the principle used today in both the United States and the Soviet Union. Tsiolkovsky called his second rocket design a squadrilla, or flying squadron. Its rockets were grouped together instead of being arranged one after the other and they all burned at once. When half of the total fuel was expended, the outer rockets transferred their remaining fuel to the inner rockets and fell off. This process was repeated until one rocket remained.

For fuel, Tsiolkovsky suggested that liquid oxygen could be combined with one or another of several substances including liquid hydrogen, alcohol, hydrocarbons, kerosene, and methane. He also suggested that rocket fuel could be used to cool the walls of a rocket's combustion chamber.

Today, the Soviet Union claims that Tsiolkovsky was years ahead of other rocket pioneers. Although the American rocket expert Robert H. Goddard had proposed a multistage rocket in 1914, the Russians say that Tsiolkovsky mentioned the possibility of such rockets before then. Likewise, they discount the fact that Tsiolkovsky, Goddard, and the German rocket pioneer Hermann Oberth all independently recognized the advantages of liquid fuel for rockets. And they contest the claim that Goddard and Count Guido von Perquet, an Austrian, both suggested the use of rocket fuels as coolants before Tsiolkovsky did.

Nevertheless, Konstantin Tsiolkovsky's contributions to rocket theory and spacecraft design are impressive. In addition to the work already mentioned, he investigated the relationship between rocket motion and exhaust velocity and weight, an equation that came to be known as the "Tsiolkovsky formula." This Russian rocket pioneer may also have been the first to design an earth satellite and a space platform, the latter to be used as a way station on future flights to the moon and the planets. He also developed a method of using solar energy for the batteries of an artificial satellite. In his writings he discussed how men could live in space vehicles and he worked out methods for such vehicles to reenter the earth's atmosphere safely.

For many years Tsiolkovsky received little recognition from his countrymen and he was unknown outside Russia. In 1914 he wrote: "How difficult it is to work for years all alone under unfavorable circumstances and not see any light or help from anywhere." Yet he continued to investigate the possibilities of rocket propulsion, and gradually his ideas gained acceptance. Eventually, the Soviet government granted him a subsidy and, later, a pension, and his writings were published at public expense. After Tsiolkovsky's death in 1935, the house at Kaluga, where he had lived and worked for forty years, became a museum. Kaluga, 90 miles southwest of Moscow, is also the site of a monument to the rocket pioneer. His statue stands before a silvery rocket on a pedestal inscribed with words Tsiolkovsky wrote in 1913: "Mankind will not remain on earth forever, but in its quest of light and space will at first timidly penetrate beyond the confines of the atmosphere, and later will conquer for itself all the space near the sun."

During the last years of his life, Tsiolkovsky's writings and diagrams were studied by many Russian scientists. One of them, Friedrich Tsander, became a disciple of the rocket pioneer. Tsander began his own rocket studies and experiments in 1908, when he was twenty-one and still a student at the Polytechnic Institute in Riga, Latvia. In fact, he became so enthusiastic about the possibilities of space travel that he named his daughter Astra and his son Mercury. Tsander corresponded with Tsiolkovsky frequently and, at the older scientist's request, edited a collection of Tsiolkovsky's writings.

Unlike Tsiolkovsky, Tsander did not carry out his rocket studies in seclusion. He traveled throughout Russia talking about the engines, rockets, rocket planes, and spaceships that he had designed and about the possibilities of space travel. He is credited with interesting a number of young scientists and engineers in rocketry and space exploration. Some of them joined the Soviet Society to Study Interplanetary Communications, which was organized in Moscow in 1924 with Tsiolkovsky and Tsander among its members. (In Russian, the term interplanetary communications is synonymous with space flight.) The Soviets claim that their society was the first such group to be organized anywhere. However, GIRD (the initials derive from the Russian words for Group for the Study of Reaction Motion), organized in 1929 with more scientists and fewer students in its membership, is generally credited with being the first really scientific rocket society to be organized in Russia. This was two years after the founding of the German Society for Space Travel.

Friedrich Tsander carried his work beyond rocket designs on paper to the actual testing of working models. His first test-stand firing produced a thrust, or propelling force, of more than 10 pounds. The rocket, which he called OR-1, burned a mixture of kerosene and liquid oxygen. In 1933 GIRD tested another Tsander rocket, the OR-2, and pronounced it a success. The OR-2 developed 110 pounds of thrust using gasoline and liquid oxygen as fuel. Tsander was working on a third rocket when he died, shortly after the OR-2 tests began.

The ORM-52, a rocket engine that was capable of producing 660 pounds of thrust, was also tested in 1933. Its designer was V. P. Glushko. The ORM-52 burned a mixture of kerosene and nitric acid. In 1935 a meteorological rocket developed by Michael Tikhonrarov, with an engine designed by L. S. Dushkin, reached an altitude of 6 miles. The rocket, which weighed 65 pounds, was 8½ feet long and 6 inches in diameter. Both Glushko and Tikhonrarov were among those who later worked on the Sputniks.

At the time when relatively little was being written in English about rockets and space exploration, the Russians published a nine-volume encyclopedia on astronautics. Finished in 1932, it was a valuable reference work for Soviet scientists. In addition to this encyclopedia, several dozen books on astronautics were published in the Soviet Union.

During World War II and the years immediately preceding it, the Russians concentrated on the largely secret development and production of military rockets. The most famous of the rockets was the Katyusha (Little Kitty). Fired from multibarreled guns, Katyusha rockets helped drive the German army back from Stalingrad and Moscow.

All of the combatants used rockets during World War II, but no other country equaled the breakthrough that Germany achieved with the V-2 (Vengeance Weapon No. 2). A rocket-powered guided missile, the V-2 was 46 feet long with a diameter of 5½ feet. Its 28,500-pound takeoff weight included 2,200 pounds of high explosives. As a propellant, the V-2's rocket engine used a mixture of liquid oxygen and ethyl alcohol. It produced 56,000 pounds of thrust. The V-2 had a 200-mile range and a top velocity of 3,500 miles per hour. It was powered only during the first sixty-five seconds after launching and then coasted the rest of the way to its target. Because the V-2 traveled faster than the speed of sound, its victims never heard it coming.

The V-2 was a high-priority project of the German government, which poured vast sums of money into its development after the German army took it over in 1933. At the Peenemünde base, a specially constructed installation on the Baltic Sea, rocket experts Walter Dornberger and Wernher von Braun headed a work force of as many as twelve thousand people. By 1942 they were able to launch an early model of the V-2. Weighing more than 14 tons, it climbed to an altitude of 54 miles. On September 6, 1944, the first combat V-2 was launched against Paris. Between that date and the end of the war in Europe eight months later, approximately 4,000 V-2's were fired, mostly against Antwerp and London.

Although the V-2 was perfected too late to affect the course of the war, Germany's accomplishment alarmed its enemies, who had nothing like it in their own arsenals. Consequently, the victors, especially the United States and the Soviet Union, searched for information about the V-2 when they entered a defeated Germany, a search that was intensified by a growing rivalry between the onetime allies.

In the part of Germany occupied by the United States Army, American intelligence teams managed to locate V-2 rockets, rocket parts, drawings, and technical data. Moreover, Dornberger, von Braun, and about one hundred and fifty other rocket experts surrendered to the American forces.

Russian soldiers captured Peenemünde, which had been largely destroyed. However, in their zone of occupation, the Russians located valuable rocket materials and a considerable number of rocket scientists and engineers, who were eventually taken to the Soviet Union where they assisted in the rebuilding of the Russian rocket program. They doubtless played an important role in the assembling of the large number of V-2's that the Russians later launched for research and training purposes.

Many people believe that the captured German experts were largely responsible for the Sputniks and other Russian accomplishments in rocketry in the years after World War II. Although they have released little information on the subject, the Russians deny this, and Wernher von Braun is one authority who believes them. After talking with his former Peenemünde colleagues who later worked in Russia, von Braun told a congressional committee: "They did not, to any appreciable extent, actively participate in the hardware phase of the rocket and missile development program in the Soviet Union."

According to one account, German rocket experts were divided into groups of about fifteen, with each group assigned to work with a larger group of Russian technicians. When a project reached a certain stage, the Russians took over and the Germans were assigned elsewhere. In this way the Russians utilized the basic knowledge of the Germans, but only their own experts were involved in advanced rocket work.

Employing what they could learn from the Germans and the

not inconsiderable abilities of their own rocket experts, the Soviets improved the V-2, an achievement that occurred also in the United States. They increased the V-2's thrust and range and started work on an even more powerful rocket engine. By 1949 the Soviet Union had begun a research program in which instruments and animals were rocketed as high as 68 miles into space and returned by parachute.

Not all of the Soviet rocket effort was directed toward scientific investigation, however. Relations between the Soviet Union and its former allies continued to deteriorate. Moreover, the Russians were alarmed by the fact that the United States had the atom bomb, a deadly weapon that could be delivered by a rocket missile. Soviet leaders were determined to develop their own nuclear warhead and a rocket powerful enough to transport it. They succeeded in doing both. As in the United States, however, the powerful rockets that were developed for military purposes were also used for space exploration.

Because the Soviet Union conducted its rocket program in the strictest secrecy, the rest of the world could only guess at what was happening in the laboratories and at the rocket bases of that vast country. There were, however, hints from time to time. In November, 1953, Academician A. N. Nesmeyanov, president of the Soviet Academy of Sciences, addressed a meeting of the World Peace Council in Vienna, Austria. During the course of a speech urging international cooperation among scientists, he said: "Science has reached a stage when it is feasible to send a stratoplane to the moon, to create an artificial satellite of the earth." In 1954 the Soviets organized an agency called the Interdepartmental Commission on Interplanetary Communications (ICIC) to direct and coordinate Russian efforts to solve the problems of mastering space. The ICIC's chairman was the noted scientist Leonid I. Sedov. The rocket expert Michael Tikhonrarov was vice-chairman, and outstanding Soviet scientists from every field made up the ICIC's membership.

In August, 1955, Academician Sedov told a group of reporters at the Sixth International Astronautical Congress in Copenhagen, Denmark: "In my opinion it will be possible to launch an artificial earth satellite within the next two years, and there is a technological possibility of orbiting artificial satellites of various sizes and weights. . . . The realization of the Soviet project can be expected in the comparatively near future. I won't take it upon myself to name the date more precisely."

Meanwhile, President Dwight D. Eisenhower had announced

United States plans to launch an artificial earth satellite during the International Geophysical Year (IGY). During the IGY, which extended from July, 1957, to January, 1959, more than fifty participating nations were going to undertake scientific studies and share the results with the others. The Soviet Union was also participating in the IGY, but had made no definite commitment to launch an earth satellite. However, a Tass report did mention that Russian scientists were working on rockets and satellites for upper atmosphere research "just as in the United States of America." It went on to say: "Now scientists are making more precise a number of conditions for successfully launching satellites."

One month before the IGY began, the Soviets announced their official rocket and satellite program. They planned to launch one hundred and twenty-five meteorological rockets from three different regions and place an unspecified number of satellites in earth orbits. Later that month, one of Russia's leading scientists stated: "Soon, literally within the next month, our planet earth will acquire another satellite. . . . The apparatus by means of which this extremely bold experiment can be realized has already been created." But nothing was said about possible launching dates.

Readers of the July and August, 1957, issues of the Soviet magazine *Radio* may have guessed that an earth satellite would be launched before long. The magazine, which was published for amateur radio "hams," carried instructions for building a shortwave radio receiver and a direction finder for tracking an artificial earth satellite. Moreover, the amateur radiomen were asked to be ready to track satellites, and they were told where to send information on the signals they picked up.

Those who were willing to predict a date for the launching of the first Soviet satellite chose September 17, 1957, the one-hundredth anniversary of the birth of Konstantin Tsiolkovsky. The day was marked by speeches honoring the rocket pioneer in Moscow and in Kaluga, but no satellite went into orbit. On October 4, however, two and a half weeks later, a beep-beep signal from space announced that Russia's and the world's first man-made satellite was indeed circling the earth.

The Soviets called their satellite Sputnik, or Fellow Traveler. It weighed 184 pounds and measured 23 inches in diameter, about the size of a basketball. And it traveled around the earth once every 96 minutes, approximately.

Sputnik 1 was launched from the rocket base near Tyuratam by a multi-stage booster. A central core stage was the one that carried

A model of Sputnik, the first Soviet artificial earth satellite, launched on October 4, 1957.

the Sputnik into orbit at a speed of approximately 1,700 miles an hour. The satellite was packed with instruments to gather and transmit information on atmospheric density, temperature, cosmic rays, and micrometeoroids. It had four 8- and 9-foot antennas, which traveled into space folded against the wall of a nose cone and opened on hinges when the cone was jettisoned.

Compared with the satellites that were orbited even a short time later, Sputnik 1 was a simple affair. Nevertheless, its launching created a worldwide sensation. The shock was greatest in the United States, where Project Vanguard, the IGY earth satellite program, had run into trouble. And the payload planned for Proj-

Various parts of the first Soviet artificial earth satellite are shown here disassembled.

ect Vanguard weighed a mere 3.25 pounds.

Sputnik 1 was still in orbit and still the object of worldwide attention when a second Sputnik joined it in space on November 3. Sputnik 2 weighed an astounding 1,120 pounds. Moreover, in addition to instruments, it carried a live passenger, a female fox terrier named Laika.

Actually, Soviet scientists had been launching dog-carrying rockets since 1951 in an effort to collect data on how the animals reacted to the conditions of space flight. The dogs, traveling in sealed containers, remained aloft only briefly before returning to earth by parachute. Laika could not be recovered, but for eight days Russian scientists received valuable data from biomedical sensors attached to the fox terrier. She traveled in a sealed container in which the temperature was controlled and the air was recirculated after excess carbon dioxide and moisture had been removed. She received a balanced diet from a special dispenser. Her body wastes were stored in a rubber reservoir. Although her movements were restricted, Laika was able to stand, lie down, and sit.

Laika's week in orbit indicated that life could survive in space

Laika, the "space dog" that spent a week in orbit aboard Sputnik 2.

at least that long. Moreover, the 14-pound dog successfully withstood the acceleration of lift-off and reacted well to prolonged weightlessness.

The next Soviet satellite to go into orbit contained only instruments, but Sputnik 3, weighing 2,925 pounds, was large enough to carry a variety of devices for collecting and transmitting data from space. Launched on May 15, 1958, it was an orbiting laboratory that investigated the earth's upper atmosphere, cosmic rays, magnetic fields, solar radiation, and the presence of micrometeoroids in space.

Before Sputnik 3 went into orbit, the United States had launched its first satellite — not the trouble-plagued Vanguard, but the 18-pound Explorer 1. Boosted into space by one of the army's Jupiter C rockets on January 31, 1958, Explorer 1 provided the first information on the Van Allen radiation belts. When Vanguard, the second United States satellite, went into orbit on March 17, 1958, it radioed back information on the size and shape of the earth.

In 1958 the Soviets were making preparations for their next big step in space exploration. The Sputniks had provided much valuable information from their earth orbits. In addition, they had tested launching, guidance, and control systems with such favorable results that Russia's scientists were convinced that a rocket could be sent to the moon.

Sending a rocket to the moon is a far more complicated undertaking than placing a satellite in earth orbit. In the latter case the primary consideration is guiding a space vehicle into the desired path at a speed approaching 18,000 miles per hour. At that velocity an object will begin to travel around the earth because its upward movement and the gravitational pull of the earth exactly balance one another. A successful moon shot also depends on the rocket attaining the desired path at the correct speed, but careful consideration must be given to the location of the earth, the moon, and the sun in relation to each other and to their gravitational effects on the rocket.

The Soviets launched their moon rocket on January 2, 1959. The first news releases referred to it as a cosmic rocket, or sometimes as Mechta, a Russian word meaning "dream," but the craft later received the designation Luna 1.

Luna's 796-pound spherical instrument canister carried devices to study the moon's magnetic field, lunar radioactivity, solar radiation, and meteoric particles in space. There were three radios to send all this information back to earth. In addition, Luna carried

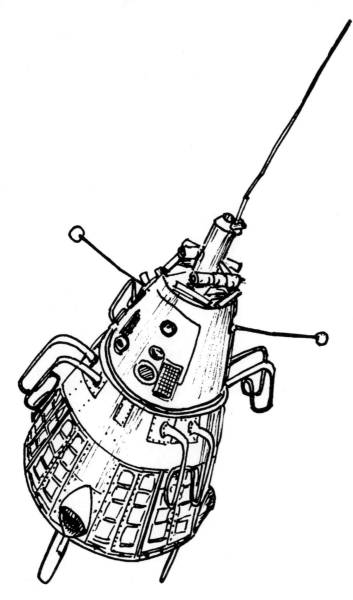

A sketch of Sputnik 3.

sodium that was emitted in the form of a 62-mile-wide sodium cloud on the second day of the moon mission to give observers on the earth an opportunity to photograph that part of the flight. Only one fairly good photo resulted, however.

Thirty-four hours after launching, Luna 1 passed within some 4,000 miles of the moon. In view of the difficulties involved in directing a rocket to the moon, this was a commendable achievement. Furthermore, Soviet scientists had never said that they expected Luna 1 to land on the moon. Instead, it continued on a journey toward the sun, a silent journey after its radios failed. It went into orbit around the sun, becoming the first artificial satellite of that body. It is still in solar orbit, circling the sun once every four hundred and fifty days.

On September 12, 1959, the Soviet Union announced that a second cosmic rocket had been launched toward the moon. The official announcement disclosed that the last stage of a multistage rocket had achieved the speed, 7 miles per second, that was required to break out of the earth's gravitational field. The rocket carried an 860-pound, ball-shaped container filled with instruments for studying the radiation around the earth, the earth's magnetic poles, cosmic radiation, micrometeoroids in space, and the magnetic poles of the moon.

Signals from the moon-bound Luna 2 were received by tracking stations in the Soviet Union and by England's Jodrell Bank Observatory, where a large radio telescope was trained toward the moon. Signals were also picked up briefly in Japan and in San Francisco in the United States. Further evidence that another moon rocket had been launched came when Luna 2 released a cloud of sodium vapor that was photographed by several Soviet observatories.

Radio stations in the Soviet Union broadcast frequent bulletins on Luna 2's progress. An early bulletin stated: "According to preliminary data, the rocket is moving along a trajectory close to the calculated one." And indeed it was. Before long, Russian rocket men were able to predict just where and when Luna 2 would land.

Approximately thirty-four hours after the launching, Luna 2's beep-beep signal stopped abruptly. The spacecraft had crashed on the moon! Its point of impact was in the predicted target area, roughly 270 miles from the center of the moon's face as seen from the earth. Russia's scientists had accomplished this feat without a midcourse correction of Luna 2's flight path; the craft had no equipment for such a maneuver.

The crash landing on the moon destroyed all of Luna 2's instruments, but it had already sent back enough data to convince Soviet scientists that the moon had neither radiation belts nor a magnetic field — or, at best, only very weak ones. The instruments and their container, the first man-made objects to reach another celestial body, had been sterilized to safeguard the moon from contamination by bacteria from the earth. Several metal pennants that Luna 2 carried to the moon were also sterilized. Some of the pennants bore the letters CCCP and the Soviet Union's coat of arms. Others were inscribed: "U.S.S.R. September 1959."

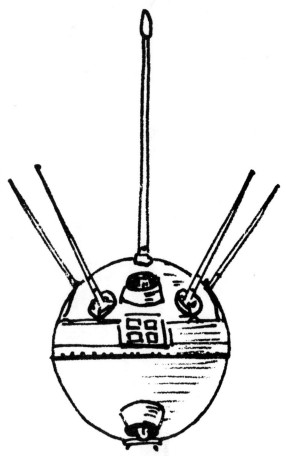

A drawing showing the basic design of Luna 1 and Luna 2.

Even as Luna 2 traveled toward the moon, Soviet scientists were readying still another cosmic rocket. They launched it on October 4, 1959, the second anniversary of the pioneering Sputnik 1. This time the official announcements stated: "The last stage of the rocket, after it attained the necessary speed, put the automatic interplanetary station into the required orbit." Luna 3 was going to orbit the moon!

Luna 3 carried scientific and radio equipment for what the Russians called "a broad range of scientific studies in outer space." No mention was made of lunar photography, but that turned out to be the spacecraft's primary mission.

The epochal picture-taking took place on October 7 when Luna 3 was on the moon's far side, the side that is never seen from the earth. It began with a signal from Russian scientists that stopped Luna's spinning, probably by activating small reaction jets. Once the craft was stabilized, windows at each end opened. One end, directed by a light-seeking device, swung toward the sun. A similar device in the other end lined up on light reflected from the moon. Luna 3 was now positioned in a direct line between the sun

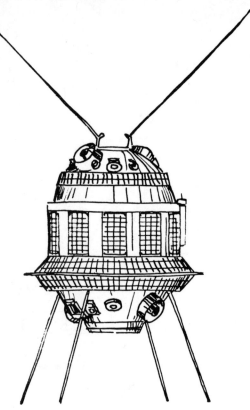

Luna 3 carried scientific and radio equipment. Its primary mission was to photograph the moon.

and the moon. From an opening pointed down at a pocked lunar surface that had never been seen by man, the craft's dual-lens, 35-mm. camera took pictures for forty minutes, covering about 70 percent of the moon's far side. The resulting photos were developed and printed by the Luna's photographic equipment and relayed to the Soviet Union from 240,000 miles in space.

While Luna 3 continued its journey in space, following a path that took it around the earth as well as the moon, Soviet scientists studied the photos the craft had taken. The photos were fuzzy, but they showed the far side of the moon to be more level than the side facing the earth. The far side contained some irregular features, however, and these the Russians proceeded to name. One depression became the Sea of Moscow; another was named the Sea of Mechta, honoring Luna 1. (Lunar depressions are called seas because seventeenth-century astronomers, using primitive telescopes, thought they looked like bodies of water.) A range of lunar mountains became the Soviet Mountains. And the largest crater was named for Konstantin Tsiolkovsky, the rocket pioneer whose theories about space travel had led to the remarkable achievements of the Sputniks and the Lunas.

3 | A SECRET SOVIET SPACE PROGRAM

Unlike the American National Aeronautics and Space Administration, which issues a steady stream of information about its projects and the people working on them, the Soviet Union's Interdepartmental Commission on Interplanetary Communications, whose membership includes some of Russia's outstanding scientists and a number of military experts, releases very little data. This forces Western observers to piece together bits of information from several sources to learn about the Soviet space program.

It appears that in the Soviet Union a single individual is in charge of each important space shot. He has wide authority to recruit people with the necessary skills and to obtain the equipment that he needs. Unlike the procedures in the United States, there is little subcontracting of parts for boosters and space capsules. Instead, one manufacturing center produces almost all of the equipment for a space mission.

The men who are in charge of the various phases of the Soviet space program are well paid by Russian standards, but they receive no publicity. Their titles may appear in news stories about space missions, but their names are never mentioned. Such secrecy is necessary, the Soviets have said, to preserve the privacy of space officials who might otherwise be in danger of assassination by Western agents.

Chief Designer Sergei Pavlovich Korolev is a good example of the secrecy that has surrounded Russia's leading spacemen. While he was alive, he was known only as the Chief Designer, or Chief Constructor, yet he played a major role in developing the Sputniks, the Lunas, the Vostok and Voskhod spacecraft, and the boosters that lifted them into space.

Korolev, who was born in 1906, seems to have displayed a talent for engineering at an early age. He was especially interested in designing airplanes, then a comparatively new field. He attended Moscow's prestigious Bauman Technological Institute and, after graduation, learned to fly to increase his understanding of aviation

Chief Designer Sergei Pavlovich Korolev, who played a major role in developing the Soviet Sputniks, Lunas, Vostoks, and Voskhod spacecraft.

engineering problems. While still a young man, he designed a successful light plane called the SK-1, the SK standing for his initials. With Sergei Ilyushin, who became one of the Soviet Union's leading aircraft designers, he built a successful glider.

Like many of Russia's leading spacemen, Korolev credits

Konstantin Tsiolkovsky with arousing his interest in rockets and space exploration. After reading some of Tsiolkovsky's articles, he visited the rocket pioneer at his home in Kaluga. A meeting with Friedrich Tsander increased Korolev's interest in rocketry. He decided to leave his job as a designer in a Moscow aviation plant to join a group of engineers who were working with rocket theory and design, a field that included jet propulsion. At this time Korolev designed a glider that, with the addition of a liquid-fuel jet engine, became the first Soviet jet. It was test-flown successfully in 1940.

After World War II, Korolev played an important part in the Russian rocket program. He helped develop powerful military rockets from the German V-2 and modified them for high-altitude scientific exploration. In 1951, one of his rockets carried the first dogs into space. In 1957, when he was in his fifties, he was in charge of the launching of the historic Sputnik 1.

Korolev held the rank of lieutenant general of aviation, but he wore civilian clothes after he entered the Soviet rocket program. According to Cosmonaut Yuri Gagarin, who greatly admired him, Korolev was a stout man of medium height. "He has a receding hairline, deep-set brown eyes, a small nose, and small, round hands," Gagarin wrote of the Chief Designer, whom he met for the first time when preparations were under way for the launching of Vostok 1.

Gagarin and the other cosmonauts worked with Korolev in the course of their training. On one occasion, Korolev outlined for

Sergei Korolev congratulates Yuri Gagarin on the completion of his first space flight in 1961.

the cosmonauts the progress that had been made in space science since the Sputniks. Later he showed them the Vostok spacecraft and helped them master its details.

Sergei Korolev was on hand for the launching of Vostok 1, and also for all the subsequent Vostok and Voskhod launchings during the next four years (although his name was never mentioned in news stories). When his own writings about space appeared in newspapers and magazines and when he spoke on the radio, he still remained anonymous. Not until he died of cancer in 1966 did his identity become known. Then he was accorded the acclaim that his anonymous role had previously denied him. He received tributes from Soviet leaders for his many contributions to space technology and a hero's burial in Moscow's Red Square. A monument honoring Korolev has been erected in Star City, the secluded Moscow suburb where the cosmonauts live.

Secrecy also surrounds the Soviet Union's launching sites. The use of the same type of rocket to launch both military and scientific space vehicles is often given as the reason why the public, especially foreigners, must be kept away from the sites.

Some things are known about Soviet launching facilities, however. The oldest site is at Kapustin Yar on the eastern shore of the Volga River south of Volgograd (formerly Stalingrad). It was built as a launching site for the rockets that carried scientific instruments and sometimes animals into space during the years before Sputnik 1 went into orbit. Components for military intercontinental ballistic missiles were also tested there. Because of its location near the Volga River, Kapustin Yar has a damp climate, not ideal for a space center's electronic equipment. Moreover, its rockets passed over populated areas where lives could be endangered by accidents. And, of course, in such a populated area, it was impossible to have secret launchings.

So, although they continued to use Kapustin Yar, the Soviets built a second cosmodrome at Tyuratam, 90 miles east of the Aral Sea. Tyuratam has a semiarid climate. Rockets launched there can be directed over an almost empty desert area, yet both water and rail transportation are available to bring the bulky rockets and other equipment to the launching complex.

Tyuratam is larger than Kapustin Yar. Cosmonaut Gherman Titov has described it as a city that isn't really a city. He recalled that on his first visit to Tyuratam he saw gantries that towered over steel and concrete buildings. Protruding concrete marked the location of underground blockhouses from which technicians con-

Korolev is shown here with Cosmonaut Gherman Titov.

trolled rocket launchings. A four-lane highway cut through the launching complex. Outside the rocket base, housing developments had been constructed for Tyuratam's many workers.

The trailblazing Sputniks, Lunas, and Vostok 1 were all launched from Tyuratam. Cosmonaut Titov, who was the backup pilot for Vostok 1, reports that he and Yuri Gagarin traveled to Tyuratam four days before the flight in a plane that also carried scientists, technicians, government officials, and officers of the Soviet Air Force. According to Titov, the air force was in charge of operations at Tyuratam.

A group of British schoolboys at the Kettering Grammar School, north of London, are credited with discovering the existence of a third Soviet launching site. Using an $80 radio, the students listened for signals from orbiting Soviet spacecraft. With the help of their science teacher, they analyzed the signals and plotted the paths of the craft. The amateur trackers became so skillful that they could tell when space capsules left orbit and reentered the earth's atmosphere. They also identified the signals that guided recovery parties to spacecraft that had landed.

After a launching in 1966, the students noticed that they were plotting a different ground trace. (A ground trace is an imaginary line on the surface of the earth that indicates an orbiting vehicle's path.) They also observed that the number of orbits was different from earlier observations, as, of course, more orbits would be required to bring the capsule back to the usual recovery area during the preferred morning hours. The boys analyzed what information they had, but it wasn't enough to tell them where the capsule had been launched.

A second launching, apparently from the same site, helped to solve the mystery. By carefully studying the ground trace of the second craft's initial orbit and noting where it crossed the one they had recorded earlier, the students identified the launch site. It was near the town of Plesetsk, about 500 miles north of Moscow.

The Soviet government has never officially acknowledged the existence of the launching site at Plesetsk, but it is thought to have come into use early in 1966. Weather, navigation, and other scientific payloads have been orbited from Plesetsk as well as satellites with military payloads.

For many years, the rockets that the Soviet Union used to launch its space shots were the subject of much speculation. Actual rockets were carefully screened from view and when a rare picture did appear, the rocket was obscured by a cover or by the smoke of launching. Since 1967, however, some Soviet launch vehicles have been placed on public display from time to time, beginning with a booster similar to the one that launched the early Lunas and carried Cosmonaut Yuri Gagarin into orbit. Called the Vostok, it had evolved from the rocket that launched the first three Sputniks, which, in turn, had been designed originally as a powerful intercontinental ballistic missile by Sergei Korolev and his colleagues.

The main stage of the Vostok booster had a central core 91.8 feet long and 9.7 feet in diameter. Surrounding the lower portion of the core were four conical-shaped engine compartments, or strap-ons. The Vostok booster had a single upper stage. It was assembled in a horizontal position and moved by rail to the launch pad, where it was raised to an upright position over a flame deflector pit. The Vostok was a ruggedly constructed booster.

3 | A SECRET SOVIET SPACE PROGRAM

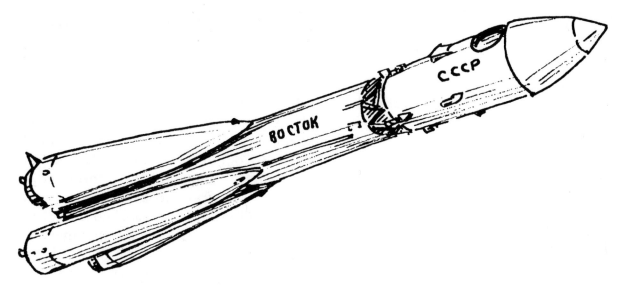

A sketch of the standard Soviet launch vehicle Vostok.

When it was horizontal, men could walk on it without doing any damage.

By improving the Vostok booster's upper stage, Chief Designer Korolev obtained a still more powerful rocket, which launched unmanned spacecraft to Venus, Mars, and the moon. It was also used to launch later manned earth-orbit missions.

Like the other components of the Soviet space program, the cosmonauts are carefully shielded from publicity. Once a cosmonaut goes into space, however, his identity is revealed and he is hailed as a national hero.

The Soviet Union began its search for cosmonauts in 1957, more than a year before a similar search got under way in the United States to find astronauts for Project Mercury. In both countries space officials looked for young men in excellent physical condition, who would be able to withstand the stresses of space flight. They wanted candidates with the right mental attitude and a good technical background. Because pilots possessed many of the qualities that would conceivably make a good spaceman, the Soviet Union made its selection from young men who were already in its air force. Project Mercury also limited its selection to military pilots, with the further requirement that they be test pilots.

Although Yuri Gagarin apparently sent off his own application for cosmonaut training, most of the cosmonauts were asked to apply after a study of their records indicated that they were highly qualified for space flight. Interviewing officers told the candidates only that they were under consideration for a mission that involved special training that would be extremely difficult and possibly dangerous. Gherman Titov was warned that the training would be backbreaking. Furthermore, he was told that it would go on night and day "until it drives you crazy." The potential cosmonaut had to make up his mind at once. He was not allowed to think the matter over before deciding to volunteer for the mysterious mission.

Of the several hundred men initially considered, the most promising received orders to report for a medical examination that lasted for several days. Although no man had as yet traveled in space, Soviet doctors were aware of some of the physical problems that the cosmonauts would encounter when they did so. The doctors were looking for the men whose bodies were best able to overcome the effects of such things as rapid acceleration and deceleration, weightlessness, vibration, noise, extreme heat and cold, and fatigue. There might also be complications arising from lack of oxygen, eating difficulties, and exposure to radiation. Psychologists were on hand to observe how the candidates reacted to discomfort and stress.

The potential cosmonauts were tested in a centrifuge that whirled them around until they were pressed into their seats by a force many times stronger than normal gravity. They endured rapid decompression in an altitude chamber, ran on a treadmill, were shaken in vibration seats, perspired in thermal rooms, and stood in icy water. When it was all over, they were sent back to their air force bases with strict orders to say nothing about the examination and its purpose. As to the results of the tests: "We will let you know later," the doctors said.

Additional tests awaited those who passed the first series, and the second series of examinations was even more difficult. Cosmonaut Titov recalled that at times he was barely able to stand and too tired to care about what the doctors thought of his performance. But Titov was in the group that survived the second elimination, as was Yuri Gagarin. Cosmonaut training began shortly afterward.

When the future spacemen reported to their new base, they found a typical military training installation with long rows of wooden barracks. There was a drill area and a well-equipped gymnasium, but no space hardware. Titov, who had expected to see launching platforms with gleaming rockets and spaceships, remarked: "We might as well have moved into a training camp for the Olympic Games."

The cosmonauts soon learned the reason for the gymnasium and the athletic equipment. During the first months of their training, they concentrated exclusively on physical exercises. They ran, they jumped, they played hockey, basketball, and other games. While they exercised, doctors observed them and the elimination process continued. Finally, only twelve cosmonauts remained of the fifty who had reported to the training camp.

Although the cosmonauts' training program resembled that of the Project Mercury astronauts in several respects, there was one big difference. The cosmonauts became skilled parachute jumpers. As pilots, they had all done some jumping, but now they learned to make difficult jumps — in bad weather and into water and hilly terrain. Each cosmonaut made between forty and fifty jumps, including extended free falls in which they did not open their parachutes until they had dropped several thousand feet. Their instructor was Nikolai Konstantovitch, the Soviet Union's most expert parachutist.

During the last part of their training, the cosmonauts concentrated on technical studies. They received classroom instruction in such basic subjects as aviation medicine, navigation, engineering, and mathematics, and progressed to the study of space medicine, rocketry, and other phases of astronautics. They also studied data and films on the launching of dogs into space in order to learn how the animals reacted to acceleration, weightlessness, and the strains of reentry into the earth's atmosphere. This is something the Project Mercury astronauts were able to do to only a limited extent. Titov reported that the cosmonauts spent hours studying the films. They observed that the worst discomfort for the space-traveling animals seemed to stem from their confinement in a small area where they were subjected to the ear-shattering noise of rocket motors. "This, too, proved encouraging," Titov wrote of this part of his training, "for the knowledge of the noise invariably strips away its effectiveness as a problem."

The cosmonauts practiced for many hours in machines called simulators that were especially designed to reproduce the conditions of space flight without ever leaving the earth. In a simulator that duplicated a spacecraft cabin, they learned to read an array of dials and use spacecraft controls. Yuri Gagarin described the simulator this way: "When seated in the cabin, the cosmonaut faced a full battery of instruments and the flashing varicolored lights needed to duplicate all possible contingencies in flight. We sent and received radio messages that were recorded on tape, made observations through portholes and optical orientation systems, did orientation by globe, and made entries in the logbook — plenty to keep us busy."

Engineers had designed the simulators so that they could reproduce the conditions of a normal flight or an emergency situation. In an emergency, the cosmonauts were expected to take the prescribed corrective measures. To make the exercises as realistic as possible, they wore full space suits, even while eating.

Another training machine was a padded metal box just big enough to hold a cosmonaut and a Vostok pilot's seat. The cosmonauts called the box the Iron Maiden. When a cosmonaut used the box he wore a space suit and he had medical sensors taped to his body. Technicians strapped him into the seat and closed the box. Then the Iron Maiden rotated in three directions at once. While it went through its unpleasant gyrations, the cosmonaut, in total darkness, was expected to provide a running report on the sensations he experienced and how he felt. Scientists developed the Iron Maiden to give the cosmonauts experience with the kind of violent tumbling they might encounter in an out-of-control spacecraft. Gherman Titov reported that the device left him with a feeling of nausea that lasted for several hours. But after repeated rides, he became accustomed to the uncomfortable three-axis motion.

To learn the effects of zero gravity, the cosmonauts rode in planes that streaked upward and then over and down in a huge arc. At the top of the arc, for up to a minute at a time, the cosmonauts would be weightless. While not very long, this was as much as could be accomplished without actually going into space.

A centrifuge reproduced for the cosmonauts the opposite of weightlessness. Whirling around at the end of a huge metal arm, while sensitive measuring devices recorded their physical condition and ability to function, they experienced many times the normal pull of gravity. During some rides they tried to identify numbers that flashed on a screen. The test began with large numbers and ended with small ones. The centrifuge helped prepare the cosmonauts for the stresses they would experience during launching and again when they reentered the earth's atmosphere. Each man was expected to sustain a force fifteen times greater than normal gravity for several minutes.

One of the cosmonauts' training devices was called the Chamber of Silence — and for good reason. No sound could penetrate its thick walls. Located in a large laboratory building, the chamber was mounted on rubber shock absorbers. It had two windows of very thick glass that could be covered from the outside and a

This still shot from a Soviet film shows cosmonauts just before reaching the stage of weightlessness.

soundproof door. In the chamber, which was equipped with a bed, a table, a Vostok pilot's seat, and a large wall board with numbered squares, the cosmonauts spent days at a time. The Chamber of Silence was designed to test their emotional stability when confined in a small space and completely shut off from the rest of the world.

Cosmonaut Gagarin referred to a stay in the chamber as "solitary confinement." He noted that a cosmonaut was never told how long his stay would be. Gherman Titov, who on one occasion remained in the chamber for a record fifteen days, confessed that he did not like that part of his training. "The silence crashed against me with what seemed to be physical force," he reported.

During his early visits to the chamber, Titov performed various tasks such as reading from technical manuals and newspapers and solving mathematical problems for the doctors in charge. Later, however, he was told to sit in the Vostok seat without moving or talking. The cosmonaut had to overcome an almost irresistible urge to cry out — to make some sound to break the overwhelming silence. He found that it helped to concentrate hard on the world outside the chamber and he passed the test successfully. But when the door of the chamber finally opened, even normal voices sounded like explosions.

When Cosmonaut Titov remained in the Chamber of Silence for fifteen days, he occupied a Vostok seat that had been fitted with spaceship control equipment. A Vostok instrument panel had been installed around the seat. During the test, the instruments simulated a Vostok orbital flight and the cosmonaut was expected to respond and to communicate with ground technicians as if a flight were actually in progress.

Although he had a schedule to follow, Titov found that the hours dragged by slowly in the silent chamber. He recalled that he mentally took apart an automobile and put it back together again. He also reviewed all the technical manuals and textbooks he had studied; and he sang, whistled, or hummed every song he could remember. His feelings when the door finally opened, he said, were "beyond description."

The cosmonauts had to endure other uncomfortable tests, although none was as troublesome as the Chamber of Silence. They practiced in a vibration stand that reproduced the shaking of a spaceship when rocket engines were in operation. In a thermal chamber they endured high and low temperatures for considerable periods. Wearing complete space suits, they were submerged in a deep-water tank to test the suit and its breathing apparatus.

Not until fairly late in their training did the cosmonauts inspect the Vostok spaceship. They had studied drawings of the ship and its equipment, but they had never actually seen the craft in which some of them were going to orbit the earth.

One morning the cosmonauts were taken to what Gherman Titov called "an air force engineering center." It was heavily guarded; admission, even for the cosmonauts, was by pass only. There, in a huge hangar, they saw the Vostok for the first time. The silver spaceship seemed to sparkle under the arc lights that illuminated the hangar. Titov recalled later that he thought the Vostok was "beautiful." For all of the cosmonauts, it was an impressive sight.

Chief Designer Korolev had joined the cosmonauts for their

first visit to the Vostok. As they stood at the bottom of a metal stairway that led to the spaceship, the Chief Designer said: "Go on, she's all yours."

Twelve eager cosmonauts rushed up the stairs. Titov, in the lead, was the first to climb into the Vostok. He settled into the pilot's seat, touched the controls, studied dials and switches. Before he had finished his examination, the other cosmonauts were clamoring for their turn. Reluctantly, Titov relinquished the pilot's seat to the next man in line, Yuri Gagarin.

The cosmonauts had other opportunities to study the Vostok in the days that followed. They also were allowed to make suggestions for the modification of spacecraft instruments and controls. Titov, who had considerable engineering skill, thought that the illumination of the spacecraft's dials could be improved and that one of the controls was difficult to use. Other cosmonauts also had recommendations for improvements and some of their suggestions were incorporated into the spacecraft. One of the changes involved the pilot's seat; as a result of a suggestion, it was mounted on bearings to enable it to turn in a complete circle, an improvement that pleased all the cosmonauts.

While they were working with the Vostok, the cosmonauts learned that Yuri Gagarin would be the first to take the craft into space. Gherman Titov was to be Cosmonaut No. 2. They had been tentatively selected some time previously and their training was adjusted to meet the needs of their particular flight. The other cosmonauts had also received provisional assignments, although only Gagarin's and Titov's assignments were announced. With this announcement, the Soviet manned space program entered a new phase.

4 | TWENTY-FIVE HOURS IN ORBIT—GHERMAN TITOV AND VOSTOK 2

In the spring of 1960, the cosmodrome at Tyuratam bustled with activity. Preparations were under way for a series of launchings that would pave the way for man's first venture beyond the earth's atmosphere. On May 15, Spacecraft 1, the first of the series, left Tyuratam. Inside its 5,512-pound pressure cabin was a dummy cosmonaut. The spacecraft went into a circular orbit 188 miles high, and while it traveled around the earth, Chief Designer Sergei Korolev and his men carried out a number of successful experiments. They failed to accomplish one of their important objectives, however. The spacecraft did not return to earth. During the sixty-fourth orbit, after the cabin containing the dummy had separated from the rest of the spacecraft in response to an electronic command from the earth, stabilizing jets failed to work properly. Instead of heading toward the earth's surface, the spinning cabin went into a higher orbit.

Chief Designer Korolev was disappointed that Spacecraft 1 could not be recovered, but he did not think it necessary to repeat its mission. He moved on to Spacecraft 2, which, on August 19, carried into orbit two dogs, named Belka and Strelka, forty mice, two rats, insects, plants, seeds, microbes, another dummy cosmonaut, and a two-camera television system.

Spacecraft 2, which closely resembled the man-carrying Vostok, went into an orbit that ranged from 189 to 210 miles above the earth. While it sped along its orbital path, the spacecraft's camera recorded the reactions of Belka and Strelka and their companions. The cosmonauts were to spend many hours studying what Gherman Titov called "fascinating" films of the animals floating about in zero gravity.

After more than twenty-five hours in orbit, Spacecraft 2 successfully reentered the earth's atmosphere. At an altitude of approximately 21,000 feet, the passenger compartment separated from the rest of the craft and completed the descent suspended under huge parachutes. It landed only 7 miles from the intended target area with its contents in good condition.

Three and a half months later Spacecraft 3 left the launching pad at Tyuratam. It carried two canine passengers, named Pshchelka and Mushka, and a number of other small animals, as well as insects and plants. Spacecraft 3 had been equipped with a new Vostok control system, but otherwise it resembled Spacecraft 2 and followed a similar orbital path.

After a day in orbit, all of the tasks planned for Spacecraft 3 had been completed and ground controllers sent a signal to return the satellite to earth. The craft's retro-rockets fired to slow it down, but the new automatic control system failed to work. Spacecraft 3 reentered the earth's atmosphere too rapidly and at too steep an angle. The resulting friction turned it into a ball of fire. All that survived of Spacecraft 3 and its contents was a small amount of ash that eventually drifted down to earth.

Spacecraft 3's destruction was much more serious than the failure of Spacecraft 1 because it was a prototype of the craft that would take the first cosmonaut into space. In fact, the cosmonauts were not told about the fiery demise of Spacecraft 3 for several weeks. But when they were told they received all the details, in-

Cosmonaut Gherman Titov.

cluding the sobering fact that had a man been aboard he would have been unable to save himself. While one of their instructors explained what had happened to Spacecraft 3, psychologists watched the cosmonauts' reactions.

Gherman Titov expressed the opinion that in such an ambitious program there was bound to be a failure sooner or later. Evidently his colleagues agreed with him. One of them jokingly suggested that the scientists who had designed the faulty equipment should pay for the lost spacecraft. The idea amused the cosmonauts, and Titov noted that the psychologists seemed pleased with their response.

Undeterred by the fate of Spacecraft 3, Soviet scientists launched Spacecraft 4 on March 9, 1961. It carried a dummy pilot, a dog named Chernushka, guinea pigs, mice, insects, and seeds. While television cameras recorded the reactions of its animal passengers, the spacecraft circled the earth once and landed safely.

Just sixteen days later, with the cosmonauts watching a launching for the first time, Spacecraft 5 went into orbit. Its dog passenger, Zvesdochka (Little Star), had been named by Yuri Gagarin. The spacecraft also carried other experimental animals and a dummy pilot. Like Spacecraft 4, this craft also completed one earth orbit and landed. The missions were brief because Chief Designer Korolev had decided that the first manned spacecraft would remain aloft for a single orbit only instead of the six originally planned.

The successful flights of Spacecraft 4 and Spacecraft 5 prepared the way for the next craft to be launched from Tyuratam. It was the memorable Vostok 1 with Cosmonaut Yuri Gagarin in the pilot's seat.

Four months after Vostok 1's journey into space, Vostok 2 was ready to leave Tyuratam's launching pad. During the busy weeks between the two manned missions, Chief Designer Korolev and his assistants added new monitoring and navigational equipment to the Vostok to prepare it for a longer flight. They made only minor changes, however, because the Vostok's basic equipment had worked flawlessly for Cosmonaut Gagarin.

Gherman Titov, the 25-year-old cosmonaut assigned to Vostok 2, helped with the spacecraft's modifications. He also had his own preparations to make for the flight, which was scheduled to last for an unprecedented seventeen orbits. Moreover, for short periods, Vostok 2 was to be under the partial manual control of its pilot, something that had not been true of Vostok 1.

August 6, 1961, launch day for Vostok 2, dawned warm and clear. Earlier violent solar eruptions, whose harmful radiation could have endangered the cosmonaut, had subsided and conditions seemed perfect for the mission.

With his standby, Cosmonaut Andrian G. Nikolayev, Titov had spent the night in the cosmonauts' cottage at Tyuratam, where he had slept when he was Yuri Gagarin's backup pilot, and, as before, both men prepared for the flight. A final medical examination, calisthenics, a breakfast eaten from tubes, the attaching of medical sensors, and the donning of space suits took less than an hour. The two cosmonauts rode to the launching pad together and parted at the base of the gleaming Vostok rocket. "Good luck to you, Gera," said Nikolayev.

After a brief prelaunch ceremony, Gherman Titov entered his spaceship. The countdown, already under way, proceeded without a hitch. Titov's checklists were brief. He had time to glance around the cabin, to admire Vostok 2's banks of instruments and luminous dials. He noted the colored globe, about 5 inches in diameter, that would rotate with the earth to tell him where he was at any given time. An ingenious speedometer would register the number of revolutions the Vostok made around the earth. The polished black handle with which he would maneuver the spaceship was within easy reach.

Cosmonaut Titov has written that he had been sealed inside Vostok 2 only twenty minutes when he received a ten-minute warning. Through his earphones he could hear the clipped phrases of the technicians in the control room as they went through the last steps of the countdown. Finally, a calm voice announced: "Sixty seconds." With his eyes on the sweeping second hand of the Vostok's clock, Titov braced himself in the well-padded pilot's seat. He heard the powerful rocket engines roar to life beneath him. The lift-off came at exactly 9:00 A.M.

As Vostok 2 shot skyward, the cosmonaut felt as though an enormous weight was pushing against his body. He could still move, however. He pressed a button to uncover a porthole through which he could see a rapidly shrinking earth. "All's well," he radioed the Tyuratam control room.

"Eagle, Eagle," the control room replied, "this is Spring One. We are following your flight, receiving your transmission loud and clear. Good luck!"

Eagle was Titov's call sign during the flight of Vostok 2. Ground Control's call sign was Spring One.

While he maintained radio contact with the control room, Titov was monitoring his instruments and watching the everdiminishing earth beneath him. He could identify plowed fields, forests, and mountains. "Colors were quite extraordinary and the light in the cabin seemed to have passed through stained glass," he reported later.

When Vostok 2's powerful first-stage rocket exhausted its fuel and dropped off, Titov felt a momentary hesitation in the spacecraft's upward progress until the second stage took over. A third stage carried the Vostok into orbit before it, too, dropped off. Once in orbit, the pressure that had pinned the cosmonaut to his seat disappeared. Now he was weightless.

Titov's first experience with weightlessness was an odd one. He felt as though he had somersaulted and was flying through space with his feet up! Moreover, his vision was blurred. He could not read his instrument panel or distinguish between earth and sky.

The disoriented cosmonaut shook his head. That action stabilized the balancing system of his inner ear and he could see again. Medical sensors had already relayed his condition to earth, however. "Eagle, Eagle," came the urgent call. "This is Spring One. Report immediately on your condition."

Fortunately, Eagle was able to answer: "I feel magnificent, feel magnificent!"

Reassured, Spring One radioed the good news that Vostok 2's orbit was exactly as planned. Its perigee, or low point, was 111 miles above the earth's surface; the apogee, or high point, was 160 miles. The spacecraft's speed, 17,750 miles an hour, would take it around the earth every 88.6 minutes.

To the orbiting cosmonaut, the earth looked like something out of a fairy tale. He saw what he described as "a planet enveloped in a blue coating and framed with a brilliant, radiant border." The sun was unbelievably bright. Titov switched off the Vostok's cabin lights, but in a few minutes he had to turn them on again when the spaceship plunged into darkness on the night side of the earth. Now he saw huge stars that sparkled like diamonds in a black velvet sky.

Titov had brought with him into space a detailed timetable that told him when to eat, sleep, exercise, and contact Ground Control and when to carry out a number of special assignments. Near the end of his first orbit the cosmonaut began preparations to take over manual control of the Vostok. While he would not be able to alter the spaceship's course, he could fire reaction jets to change its attitude — pitch it up or down, roll it one way or the other, and move its nose to the right or left.

As Titov's hand closed over the manual control handle he felt anxious, he wrote later. No one had ever done such a thing before. "Be cautious in your first control attempts," the Chief Designer had warned him. Titov wondered if the spaceship would obey his commands. It did, and the cosmonaut felt as though he was indeed the captain of a remarkable ship. "Vostok responds to manual controls very well," he reported to Ground Control.

Vostok 2 flew into a dawn that began with a bright orange strip on the horizon. Above this, all the colors of the rainbow glowed, and then the golden ball of the sun appeared. Below him the cosmonaut could see mountains, rivers, and clouds that threw blue shadows on the earth.

When the completion of its first orbit brought Vostok 2 back over the Soviet Union, Cosmonaut Titov radioed: "The flight is progressing successfully. All the equipment of the ship is functioning normally. I am feeling well."

Among the radio messages beamed to the cosmonaut as he flew over his homeland was one from Premier Nikita Khrushchev, who said: "All of the Soviet people are happy at the successful flight and are proud of you."

On a later pass over the Soviet Union, Titov received a message from his good friend Yuri Gagarin. The first man to orbit the earth radioed: "I am with you with all my heart. . . . I am following your flight with greatest excitement."

While radio messages flashed back and forth, sensors attached to the cosmonaut's body relayed information about his physical condition to Ground Control. At the same time television pictures transmitted from the spaceship allowed doctors in the control room to see for themselves how Eagle was faring.

As it traveled around the earth, Vostok 2 sent an almost continuous stream of information to the ground. When it was beyond the range of tracking stations in the Soviet Union or the tracking ships waiting on the world's oceans, voice messages and data on the spacecraft and its occupant were stored on tape to be fed to the first Soviet station that came within range.

From his observation post far above the earth, Cosmonaut Titov noted that the continents differed from one another in their colors as well as their outlines. Africa, for example, was a predominately yellow continent, sprinkled with dark green spots represent-

Gherman Titov is shown here on a TV screen while taking pictures with his camera during the space flight.

ing jungles. Of the oceans and seas, he thought that the ultramarine Mediterranean was the most beautiful of all.

With his hand-held Konusass camera, Titov attempted to capture some of the colors that amazed him with their brilliance. The photographs he took through Vostok 2's portholes turned out well, as did the pictures he snapped of his logbook suspended in the cabin and of himself winking at the camera.

Titov's schedule, which he followed carefully, had lunch listed for Vostok 2's third orbit. The cosmonaut recalls that he wasn't particularly hungry and would have preferred to skip the meal altogether, but eating was an important part of his program for testing the effects of weightlessness. Most of Vostok 2's food supply was packaged in tubes. The cosmonaut selected tubes containing soup puree, meat and liver paste, and currant juice. He held the tubes to his mouth and squeezed as he would have squeezed a tube of toothpaste. The contents of the tubes tasted like real food, however. With the meat and liver paste he ate several bite-sized rolls. By placing an entire roll in his mouth, he avoided scattering bread crumbs around the Vostok's cabin, where they would float indefinitely.

While Titov was drinking the currant juice, several drops leaked from the tube. The red drops hung like berries in front of his face, floating in the gravity-free cabin with a slight quivering motion. The cosmonaut scooped them into his mouth with no trouble at all. "In the main," he reported, "eating and drinking in space was as easy as on the earth."

Shortly after the completion of the spacecraft's initial orbit, Radio Moscow announced that Vostok 2 had been launched successfully. After the announcement, Titov heard reports of his flight as he passed over the world's nations. Even when he didn't understand what was said, he recognized the word Vostok, his own name, and the name of Premier Khrushchev.

From time to time the orbiting cosmonaut radioed greetings to the people below him. His flight took him over several large cities. With the aid of his navigational globe, he identified some shimmering lights as coming from Rio de Janeiro, Brazil. He also passed over Edinburgh, Scotland; Lima, Peru; Canton, China; Washington, D.C.; and Pittsburgh, Pennsylvania. Vostok 2 was seen twice in the night sky over Pittsburgh where it was reported to resemble a very bright star.

Most of the time, however, Titov looked down on the earth's vast unpopulated areas. He saw the rugged Himalayas, whose high peaks and deep valleys he described as "stacks of straw interspersed with bluish crevices." The Sahara appeared to be "an ocean of golden brown sands." The Indian Ocean was a "rich indigo blue," the Gulf of Mexico, a "startling salad-green color."

To the cosmonaut's naked eye, the Atlantic and Pacific oceans looked flat, but when he used an optical device with three- and five-power magnification, he could see waves moving across the surface of the water.

One of the cosmonaut's duties was to keep a log in which he recorded his impressions of what he saw as well as a technical account of the flight. He held the logbook on his knee; if he let go, even for a second, the book drifted away. A string secured a pencil to the logbook, which had the coat of arms of the Soviet Union on its cover. Titov said later that he had so much to write about that he had difficulty getting it all down.

In addition to serving as a record of the mission, the logbook would give scientists a chance to examine the cosmonaut's handwriting for possible effects of weightlessness. Titov, an indifferent penman, observed that his writing in space was no worse than it was on earth.

During Vostok 2's sixth orbit, Titov took over the spaceship's controls again. "This time I was more confident, since I knew what the behavior of the ship would be," he has written. "It obeyed my wishes like a well-trained animal." The cosmonaut smoothly manipulated the 5-ton spaceship, moving its nose to the left and right and up and down and swinging the craft around on its axis. After twenty minutes he regretfully returned spacecraft control to the automatic system.

Dinnertime on Vostok 2 found the cosmonaut consuming more tubes of meat paste and currant juice. Once again he admitted to not being very hungry. Moreover, he was beginning to feel tired. Titov had been orbiting the earth for more than eight hours. During that time he had traveled 148,000 miles and seen things that only one other man had ever looked at before: red-orange sunsets moving across the earth, explosive sunrises of dazzling brilliance, occurring, like the sunsets, every forty-five minutes, and other sights equally impressive. At one point Titov was so overwhelmed by the wonders of space flight that he replied to a radio call from Ground Control not with the usual formal acknowledgment, but by crying out: "I am Eagle! I am Eagle!"

Along with increasing fatigue, the Soviet Union's second spaceman was beginning to experience periods of dizziness and nausea. He had completely recovered from his initial disorientation, but now his long stay under zero-weight conditions had again affected the delicate balancing system of the inner ear. Normally, gravity influences the otoliths of the inner ear to make them change position whenever the position of the head changes. A message is then transmitted through the central nervous system to the muscles required to keep the body in balance. In Titov's case, the absence of gravity had disrupted the system, and he was having difficulty maintaining his sense of balance. He discovered that his dizziness and nausea grew worse when he moved his head or watched a rapidly moving dial on Vostok 2's instrument panel. The well-trained cosmonaut noted his symptoms in the logbook and reported them to Ground Control. "These reactions at no time interfered with the performance of my duties as they were scheduled," he later wrote of his problem.

Understandably, Titov looked forward to the sleep period scheduled for the seventh orbit. He was the first man to attempt to sleep in space. The cosmonaut sent a good-night message as he

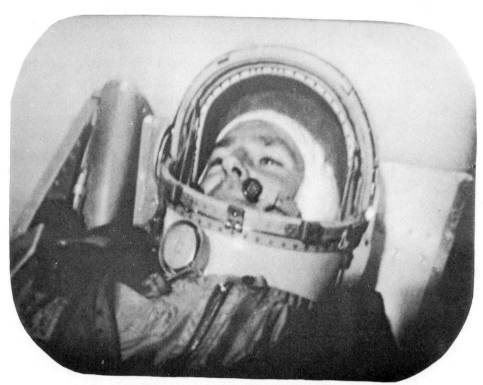

"I am eagle!" Titov radioed back to earth in his enthusiasm over space flight. Soviet scientists conducted uninterrupted observation of the cosmonaut during the mission.

flashed over Moscow: "I beg to wish you, dear Muscovites, goodnight. I am turning in now. You do as you please." It was 6:15 P.M., Moscow time, and the spaceman was scheduled to sleep until 2:00 A.M. First, however, he arranged with Ground Control to discontinue all except emergency radio messages. That done, he adjusted his restraining belts, moved his seat to a bed position and went to sleep.

About an hour later the tired cosmonaut woke up to find his weightless hands hanging in midair because he had neglected to secure his arms beneath a restraining belt. He readjusted his belts and went back to sleep. He awoke two more times, but each time sleep returned quickly. "Sleeping was fine in space," Titov reported later. "There was no need for turning over from time to time because neither hands nor legs could go numb. It was something like lying on a sea wave."

The cosmonaut slept so well that he failed to wake up on time. His dizziness and nausea had almost vanished, but according to Vostok 2's timetable he was thirty minutes behind schedule. The spacecraft was over the Pacific Ocean somewhere between Australia and the United States when Titov hurriedly began his morning activities. After reporting his instrument readings, he performed the exercises that had been especially developed for him. He stretched his arms and legs, flexed his muscles, clenched and unclenched his fists, and pulled against the belts that held his body to the pilot's seat. "These special exercises activated my heart and generally envigorated my body," Titov explained later.

During the next orbits, the cosmonaut carried out routine assignments, which he later compared to the work a pilot does on an extended cross-country flight. The striking beauty of space continued to impress him, and from time to time he took a few minutes to note his observations in the logbook.

With the beginning of the seventeenth orbit, routine flight ended. It was time for the cosmonaut to prepare for the precarious plunge from space back to earth.

For Titov, landing would be unusually hazardous. Yuri Gagarin had made a comfortable landing inside the Vostok, but the Soviet Union's second cosmonaut was going to test another landing system. He was to be catapulted from Vostok 2 to land under his own parachute.

"Are you ready for the landing?" Ground Control asked the cosmonaut.

"Ready!" he radioed back.

Titov recalled later that he felt a longing to return to earth. "It's all very well in outer space, of course," he has written, "but there's no place like home."

At the scheduled time, Vostok 2's retro-rockets fired against the line of flight to slow the spaceship. Inside the cabin, Titov could feel the vibration of the firing. Responding to the loss of speed, Vostok 2 left its orbit and headed earthward. For the cosmonaut, weightlessness disappeared to be replaced by the mounting g-forces of deceleration. Limbs that had moved effortlessly now could be moved only with tremendous effort.

Even greater changes were taking place outside the spacecraft as it dropped through the thickening atmosphere. Titov described it as a "baptism of fire." He had decided not to cover the Vostok's portholes. Now he noted a pink halo around the rapidly descending craft. The pink grew deeper, turning red, then crimson, then scarlet. Varicolored flames streaked past the portholes and the glass turned yellow. The cosmonaut inside the falling, burning spaceship remained calm, however. "I was sure nothing would happen," he wrote later. "The heat protection of the vessel had been checked and rechecked many times in previous test flights." And throughout the fiery descent, the temperature in the Vostok cabin remained a comfortable 71.6 degrees Fahrenheit.

When his instruments told him that Vostok 2 had reached the lower atmosphere, Titov prepared to eject from the spacecraft. He activated several switches, gripped his seat firmly, and watched the sweeping hand of the chronometer. A red light flashed on the instrument panel. Explosive charges hurled the cosmonaut, still in his seat, away from the spaceship. Then another device pushed him from the seat and a bright orange parachute opened above his head.

Below him, the cosmonaut could see fluffy cumulus clouds and Vostok 2 drifting to earth beneath its own white parachutes. The cosmonaut recognized the Volga River and the cities of Saratov and Engels. In the countryside he saw men working in the fields and cows grazing. He also saw a moving train. All I need now is to land on the top of a railway car, he thought.

The cosmonaut landed on the soft ground of a plowed field, however. He glanced at his watch. It was 10:18 A.M., Moscow time. His space trip had lasted 25 hours and 18 minutes!

Like Cosmonaut Gagarin, Titov had come down in the Soviet Union's recovery area to the west of Tyuratam. Cheering men and women who had observed his descent reached him first, followed by the official recovery parties. Before starting out for recovery headquarters, the cosmonaut visited the heat-blackened Vostok 2, which had landed nearby. He drank some water from the spacecraft's supply and retrieved his logbook. Then he left the landing area at the head of an impromptu motorcade.

At the recovery headquarters, jubilant officials waited to greet the returned space traveler. His fellow cosmonauts arrived to offer their congratulations and Soviet Premier Khrushchev telephoned from Moscow. "All equipment and installations in the spaceship worked perfectly. I have landed in the designated region, where I was received well. My condition is excellent," Titov told the premier.

After he had completed detailed postflight briefings, Gherman Titov went to Moscow. He met Premier Khrushchev and received a hero's welcome from thousands of Soviet citizens, who jammed Red Square to catch a glimpse of their second spaceman.

Russian scientists, who had launched Vostok 2 to investigate the effects on the cosmonaut of prolonged orbital flight and the subsequent return to earth, announced that they were pleased with

Thousands of Muscovites lined the route to Red Square to greet Titov after his historic flight.

the results of the mission. Postflight examinations revealed no adverse changes in Titov's physical or mental state. Moreover, he had been able to carry out all of his assigned tasks during his more than twenty-five hours in space.

There was one unresolved question, however. The cosmonaut had suffered from dizziness and nausea during his journey. Would that happen to every spaceman who experienced weightlessness for many hours? Or did it result from an individual reaction of Titov's? The answer would only come from more long space flights.

5 | SPACE COMPANIONS

A year passed before the Soviet Union sent another cosmonaut into space. During that year, Soviet scientists launched seven unmanned earth satellites of a type that they called Cosmos. Meanwhile, in the United States, Project Mercury orbited two manned spacecraft. The astronauts, John H. Glenn, Jr., and M. Scott Carpenter, each circled the earth three times in February and May, 1962, respectively.

In the months preceding the launching of Vostok 3, the cosmonauts continued their training, and Chief Designer Korolev worked to improve the Vostok. Like the Project Mercury spacecraft, the Vostok underwent constant changes as problems were corrected and technicians developed more advanced equipment.

Andrian Gregoryevich Nikolayev, Vostok 2's backup pilot, watched the changes in the spaceship with special interest. He was the cosmonaut who had received the coveted assignment to take the next Vostok into orbit.

The Soviet Union's third cosmonaut was thirty-two years old. He was a Chuvash, that is, a native of the Soviet Union's Chuvash Autonomous Republic, located in the central part of the country. Andrian, the son of a farmer, saw his first airplane when he was seven. For many weeks he talked of nothing but airplanes and his intention to fly one someday. Later, however, he decided to become a doctor and entered medical school. After, he transferred to a forestry school and graduated as a technical forester.

In 1950 the future cosmonaut entered the army. He was a radio operator and a machine gunner before qualifying for aviation training. As a pilot, he distinguished himself by landing a dangerously crippled jet instead of parachuting to safety and letting the plane crash. Nikolayev was observed calmly recording what had gone wrong with the plane as he walked away from the forced landing. Gherman Titov once said of his fellow spaceman: "Cosmonaut Andrian Nikolayev is the embodiment of composure, which is necessary for the commander of a spaceship. My friend is a man of iron endurance and courageous determination."

Cosmonaut Andrian Nikolayev, pilot of Vostok 3.

Cosmonaut Nikolayev amazed his colleagues with his ability to withstand long hours in the Chamber of Silence. His record was ninety-six hours, next to Titov's the longest stay of any of the cosmonauts. While enduring the silence and other discomforts of the isolation chamber, Nikolayev painted pictures that Titov has described as "beautiful." During special heat tests in the chamber, the amateur artist kept cool by painting pictures of ski slopes and blizzards. The doctors monitoring the tests were impressed with his ability to maintain his body temperature psychologically.

Vostok 3, with Andrian Nikolayev in the pilot's seat, was launched at 11:30 A.M., Moscow time, on August 11, 1962. Cameras recorded the launching for Russian television audiences and the same film was shown on a network news program in the United States a few days later.

What American viewers saw was the blurred figure of Cosmonaut Nikolayev as he climbed some ladderlike steps leading to the Vostok. The camera moved from the cosmonaut to a circular hatch, but only a small portion of the space capsule appeared in the film. Cameras also recorded the blast-off of the long, slender Vostok rocket. Viewers could clearly see the trail of fire that followed the rocket as it rose from the billowing smoke of the launching pad into a partly cloudy sky.

Vostok 3's television system and other reporting devices told Ground Control that Cosmonaut Nikolayev had successfully survived the stresses of launching and the transition to weightlessness. Once in orbit, the cosmonaut began sending radio messages to earth. His call sign was Sokol, the Russian word for falcon, or bird of prey. "I feel well," he reported. "Everything is normal on board. The earth is clearly visible through the porthole."

Traveling at a speed of 18,000 miles an hour, Vostok 3 circled the earth every 88.5 minutes. Its orbit was 156 miles from the earth at the farthest point and 114 miles at the closest.

When he passed over the Soviet Union at the beginning of the Vostok's fourth orbit, the cosmonaut exchanged messages with Premier Khrushchev. Nikolayev radioed: "I feel fine. All systems of the ship are functioning perfectly."

The premier replied: "I am glad that you feel well. I am proud of the courage you have displayed in making this flight."

Vostok 3 was also transmitting television pictures to earth, which were shown later by Russian stations. During one program,

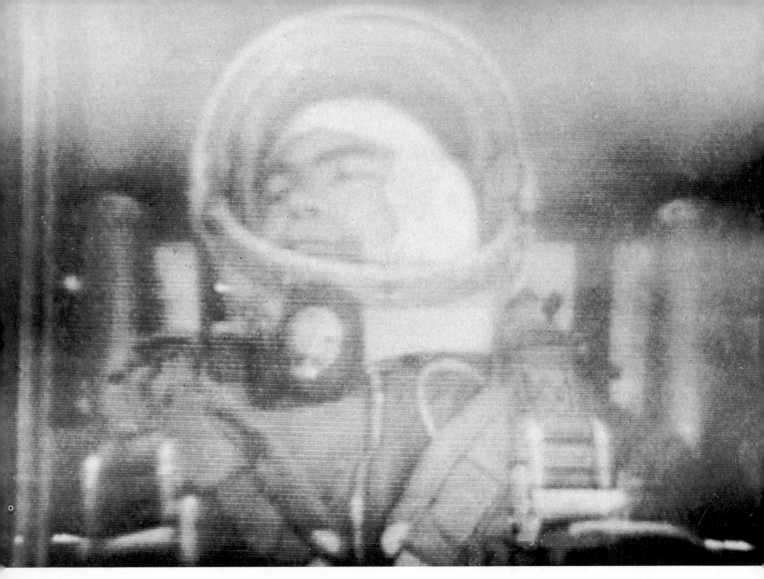

A TV shot of Cosmonaut Nikolayev in the cabin of Vostok 3, on August 11, 1962.

television audiences saw a smiling cosmonaut tying a weightless, floating ribbon around what appeared to be a logbook.

Soviet citizens were pleased to have another cosmonaut in orbit. An employee of Moscow's central telegraph office told a reporter: "I'm thrilled at the news. It is the dream of every Soviet girl and boy to fly into the cosmos like our Gagarin, Titov, and Nikolayev."

As they gathered in groups to discuss what they had heard on the radio and seen on TV, Russians speculated on the length of Nikolayev's flight. Radio Moscow had announced that the cosmonaut had gone into orbit to obtain more information on the effects of weightlessness and other space flight conditions. The flight would also test improvements in the Vostok. Almost every-

Direct telecasts by the cosmonauts from orbital space were watched by millions of people — Soviets and other nationalities around the globe. Here Muscovites watch Cosmonaut Nikolayev on their home screens during his flight.

one thought that Cosmonaut Nikolayev would stay in space longer than Titov's twenty-five hours.

Western observers, too, thought that the new Vostok might remain in orbit for a long time. They pointed out that one of the unmanned Cosmos craft had circled the earth for seventy-two hours. An equally long space flight by Vostok 3 might well be part of the Soviet Union's preparations for a manned flight to the moon. However, in its news bulletins, the Soviet government said nothing about how long the Vostok would remain in orbit or about any special experiments that were planned for the mission. As it turned out, Vostok 3 was part of a very special space mission indeed.

Radio Moscow made the exciting announcement on August 12: "The Vostok 4 spaceship, piloted by Pilot-Cosmonaut Pavel Popovich, has been set in orbit of the earth at 11 hours 2 minutes, Moscow time, today." The announcer went on to explain that Vostok 4 had been launched into an orbit close to Vostok 3's orbit to obtain experimental data on the possibility of establishing contact between the two ships. Space officials were also going to see if the actions of the cosmonauts could be coordinated and if identical conditions of space flight had the same effect on two individuals. "All systems aboard the Vostok 3 and Vostok 4 spaceships are functioning normally," the announcer assured his listeners.

Vostok 4's launching into an orbit near that of Vostok 3 tested the skill of Soviet scientists. They had to track Vostok 3 with great accuracy and carefully plan Vostok 4's launch time, flight path, and velocity to bring the new satellite close to Vostok 3. Even the smallest error would result in many thousands of miles of separation between the orbits of the two ships. Since the Vostoks lacked rocket equipment that would enable the cosmonauts to change orbits, a mistake could not be corrected once Vostok 4 left Tyuratam.

Just how well the scientists had done their work became evident when Vostok 4 began to circle the earth on a path very similar to the one followed by Vostok 3. The new Vostok's orbit was 158 miles from the earth at its farthest point and 112 miles at the closest. Moreover, the angle between the plane of Vostok 3's orbit and the plane of the equator was 64.59 degrees; for Vostok 4 it was 64.57 degrees. Both craft traveled at a speed close to 18,000 miles an hour.

Soon after Vostok 4 went into orbit, Cosmonaut Nikolayev in Vostok 3 picked up a radio signal from the new arrival. Nikolayev responded with: "Everything goes fine. I hear you perfectly. I am in a wonderful mood."

"I see the earth in clouds," Popovich told his fellow cosmonaut. "To the right from the porthole. I see the very black sky. My mood is wonderful. Everything is fine."

The Soviet Union's newest space traveler was a thirty-one-year-old Ukrainian with a reputation for cheerfulness. As a youth he attended a vocational school and an industrial-technical school before entering the Soviet Army. Later he transferred to the air force and became a fighter pilot. At one time Popovich's wife, a civilian pilot, had more hours in the air than her military pilot husband.

Cosmonaut Pavel Popovich is shown here just prior to the lift-off of Vostok 4.

Pavel Popovich was the first man to report for duty as a cosmonaut. He had greeted Yuri Gagarin, Gherman Titov, and Andrian Nikolayev when they arrived at the cosmonaut training camp and assisted them in getting settled.

During Cosmonaut Popovich's first circuit of the earth in Vostok 4 the distance between it and Vostok 3 steadily decreased. The cosmonauts were in radio contact with each other and with Ground Control as their ships drew closer together. Approximately ninety minutes after Vostok 4's launching the two ships were within sight of one another. The cosmonauts radioed the happy news to Ground Control and shortly afterward Radio Moscow announced that the spaceships had begun "group flight." The announcement did not mention the distance that separated the two craft, but it was revealed later that they had come within 4 miles

A portrait of veteran Cosmonaut Pavel Popovich, first to report for duty in the Soviet space program as a cosmonaut trainee.

of each other at the closest point. After that the gap between them widened because of the slight variation in the size of their orbits.

With the group flight of Vostok 3 and Vostok 4, Soviet scientists had come remarkably close to launching two spaceships into duplicate orbits, and the rest of the world was quick to praise their accomplishment. Sir Bernard Lovell, the director of Britain's Jodrell Bank Observatory where signals from the orbiting craft had been picked up by a huge radio telescope, said: "The two flights will do a great deal to explore communication between vehicles in space and navigation in preparation for subsequent attempts to rendezvous in space." A French newspaper carried the story under the headline: "Fantastic!"

When he learned that the Soviet Union had launched two Vostoks that had orbited within sight of one another, American Astronaut Scott Carpenter exclaimed: "Wow! Another ship in sight! That's quite a feat. I'm sure it would be an exciting thing to be able to see and hear a fellow traveler in space."

In Japan, stories of the dual flight dominated the front pages of the newspapers. "If the first rendezvous becomes a reality," one article speculated, "the Soviet Union will have made a great step forward in its moon flight program."

Japanese reporters were not the only ones who thought the Russians might be preparing for a manned flight to the moon. Unless a rocket powerful enough to send a spacecraft all the way to the earth's satellite could be developed, Soviet scientists would have to launch a vehicle to serve as a space station. A second spacecraft could then be launched to the space station for refueling and other adjustments before proceeding to the moon. Or, perhaps, an unmanned spacecraft could be launched into orbit, to be followed with a smaller manned craft. After docking, or joining up, with the larger craft, cosmonauts could transfer to it for the trip to the moon. The rendezvous, or meeting, in space of Vostoks 3 and 4 might well be an initial attempt to see if the space station idea would work. Moreover, the Chief Designer was quoted as saying that the group flight was a significant step toward an eventual landing on the moon.

Project Apollo, the United States program for sending men to the moon, also depended on the successful development of rendezvous and docking techniques. The National Aeronautics and Space Administration (NASA) was working on a powerful rocket called the Saturn that would boost a spaceship with three astronauts to the vicinity of the moon. A smaller craft would then carry two of them to the moon's surface and, later, return them to the waiting mother ship. American scientists hoped to land astronauts on the moon by 1970, but they had not yet begun to experiment with rendezvous and docking in space.

While earthlings speculated about the Soviet Union's plans to send men to the moon, Cosmonauts Nikolayev and Popovich continued in orbit. The spacemen communicated with one another every thirty minutes, calling in turn. Once, when he caught a glimpse of Vostok 3 across miles of space, Popovich told Nikolayev that his ship looked like a very small moon in the distance.

For the remainder of August 12, the cosmonauts followed similar schedules. At 2:30 P.M., Moscow time, they had lunch and then they rested for an hour before resuming their experiments and other activities. Television cameras recorded much of what happened in Vostok 3 and 4 and some of the film was broadcast on subsequent days by Russian television stations. There was one live broadcast during the first day of the joint flight. Transmission was poor, but viewers could see the cosmonauts speaking with ground controllers and making notations in their logbooks. In Vostok 3, Nikolayev placed some tape before the camera to show how it floated in the gravity-free spaceship. By 9:30 that night both cosmonauts were asleep.

Andrian Nikolayev began his third day in space and Pavel Popovich his second, at 4:30 A.M., Moscow time. Intership conversations resumed not long afterward. Cosmonaut Popovich radioed: "This is Golden Eagle [Popovich's call sign] calling Falcon. I hear you well. The temperature is 18 degrees [centigrade], humidity 65 percent. Have you understood me well?"

Cosmonaut Nikolayev answered: "This is Falcon calling Golden Eagle. I have understood you. Everything is all right with me. The temperature is 15 degrees [centigrade], humidity 65 percent. I am feeling fine. Slept well."

And Popovich replied: "Golden Eagle calling. I am in a perfect mood, slept well, feeling marvelous."

During a day devoted to scientific observations and physiological tests, the cosmonauts noted that prolonged weightlessness had not affected their ability to work. In one experiment they removed their seat belts and floated about in their space cabins. They were trying to see if they could maintain a sense of direction. They also wanted to determine the most comfortable position for a free-floating cosmonaut.

In another experiment Cosmonaut Popovich observed air

bubbles in a tightly sealed flask two-thirds full of water. When undisturbed, the air remained in the middle of the flask, but when he shook the bottle, the large bubble split into many small bubbles only to form one large bubble again. The cosmonaut also noted that water sprayed into the gravity-free cabin formed drops that gradually moved to the walls and settled there.

In the afternoon the cosmonauts sent a joint message to the men and women who had contributed to the success of the dual space flight. The message, addressed to scientists, designers, engineers, technicians, and workers, said: "We are sincerely grateful to you for the design and manufacture of the wonderful spaceships and our excellent training for the flight. We wish you further successes in the work for the good of our beloved homeland."

At 10:00 P.M., Moscow time, the hardworking cosmonauts signed off for the night. Vostok 3 had circled the earth forty times and traveled more than 1,000,000 miles, while Vostok 4 had made twenty-four orbits of the earth and traveled 625,000 miles. During the hours the spacemen slept, ground controllers watched over the Vostoks.

The cosmonauts awoke at 4:00 A.M. to begin another day in space with nearly identical messages to Ground Control: Temperature, humidity, and pressure in the spaceships remained normal. The cosmonauts had slept well and felt fine. They were ready to begin their daily physical exercises. Then they would eat breakfast.

Vostoks 3 and 4 carried a more varied food supply than the earlier Vostoks. In addition to items packed in tubes, Nikolayev and Popovich could eat meat cutlets, roast veal, boned chicken, pastries, candy, rolls, sausages, and chocolate, food that they evidently liked. One of the many news bulletins issued during the dual mission stated that the cosmonauts enjoyed good appetites in the conditions of space flight.

Other bulletins suggested that Nikolayev and Popovich had not experienced Cosmonaut Titov's reaction to prolonged weightlessness. Perhaps the reason for this was the special training that they had received. Nikolayev and Popovich were reported to have prepared for their flight with many hours of whirling and loop-the-loop exercises. The cosmonauts' apparent well-being after two and three days in orbit encouraged space officials in both Russia and the United States who had feared that weightlessness might pose a real problem in space flight. Some scientists had speculated that it might be necessary to create an artificial gravity during long missions by rotating the spaceship.

Soviet scientists announced that they were obtaining important data from the latest Vostok mission. "Miraculous instruments" were measuring the movements of the cosmonauts' heart muscles, their breathing, their brain waves, and even, in Nikolayev's case, eye movements. Miniature silver electrodes had been placed in the outer corners of the cosmonaut's eyes. The electrodes recorded his eye movements, their speed, and the muscular effort involved.

On Nikolayev's fourth day in space, and Popovich's third, the cosmonauts continued with their research programs. Vostok 4's pilot reported that he was also keeping up with his English and physics lessons. TV viewers noted that both men had grown beards and that Nikolayev appeared to be more tired than his colleague. He was in good humor, however, and carried out his schedule with no difficulty. In one of his messages to Ground Control he said: "The earth is visible quite clearly. Have seen the moon and photographed it. . . . Everything is in order. Everything follows the program."

When Vostok 3 was over the United States, Cosmonaut Nikolayev radioed from space: "Flying over your great country, I convey from the Soviet spaceship, Vostok 3, greetings to the gifted American people. I wish peace and happiness to the people of your country."

Before going to sleep for the night, Nikolayev joined Popovich in a song about space travel called "I Believe, My Friends." The cosmonauts sang:

"I believe, my friends,
That caravans of rockets
Will speed us from star to star."

Unlike the United States, the Soviet Union did not announce in advance the duration of its space flights. Cosmonauts Nikolayev and Popovich had both been in orbit considerably longer than Gherman Titov's twenty-five hours. When would they return to earth? The question was answered on August 15. At 9:24 A.M. Vostok 3's retro-rockets fired to bring the ship out of orbit after sixty-four trips around the earth. The spacecraft had traveled more than 1,600,000 miles in ninety-four hours and twenty-two minutes.

At a news conference a few days after the end of the flight, Cosmonaut Nikolayev described his return to earth: "The deceleration forces were small at first," he recalled. "Then they increased to five or six g's; then they became even more intense. Out of the window I saw smoke at first, then flames, which changed from

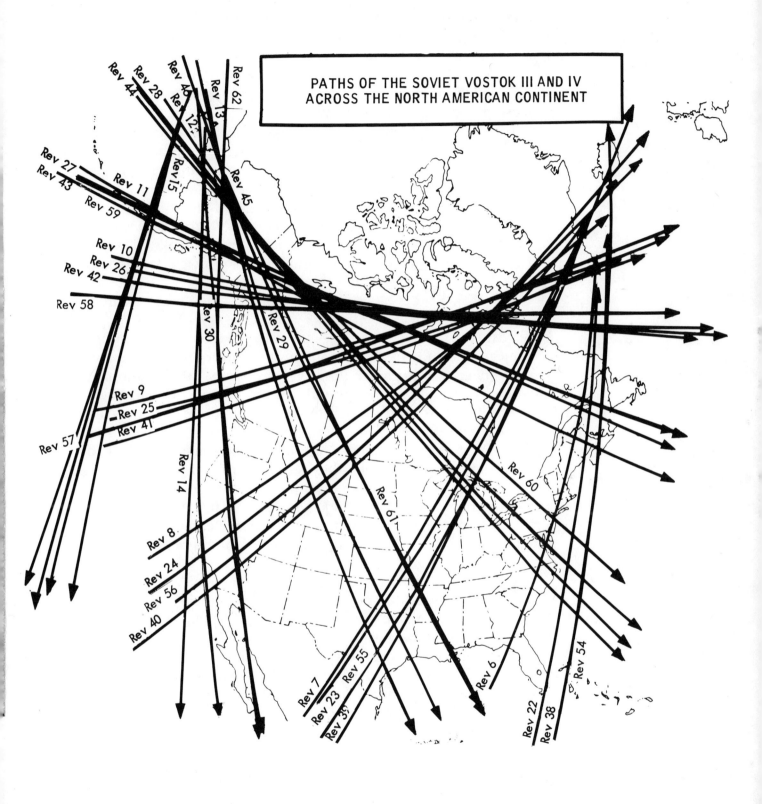

PATHS OF THE SOVIET VOSTOK III AND IV ACROSS THE NORTH AMERICAN CONTINENT

red to orange to yellow to blue. Crackling began when the flames appeared. Without my training I would have had a hard time of it. But because of my training, I was able to take the correct position and minimize the discomfort. As the deceleration forces decreased, it became like riding in a cart on a bad road. I separated from the spaceship and landed by parachute."

The cosmonaut landed in a desert area in central Kazakhstan, about 350 miles northeast of Tyuratam. A doctor with the recovery party was the first to reach him. "I stood there smiling," Nikolayev recalled. "Everything was so amazingly fine."

Cosmonaut Popovich in Vostock 4 received his landing orders at the same time that Nikolayev did. However, Vostok 4 was to begin the landing process six minutes later than Vostok 3. "Everything will be excellent. Happy returning," Popovich radioed to Vostok 3.

"Pavel, keep cool," Nikolayev replied. "Don't get excited. Everything will be okay."

Vostok 4 followed Vostok 3 to earth. Like Nikolayev, Popovich ejected from his space capsule in the lower atmosphere and landed under a large parachute. "We've done it," the cosmonaut shouted as he touched the ground. During his seventy-one hours in space he had circled the earth forty-eight times and traveled 1,230,000 miles.

Helicopters picked up the returned space travelers, who had landed some 125 miles apart. They were described as looking brisk and cheerful when they arrived at the house where they were to rest. Cosmonaut Nikolayev told the crowd that had gathered to greet them: "We thank you for your warm welcome. Look at us. The flight, as you can see, went off well. We feel fine, even wonderful."

Later, doctors confirmed that the long flights of Vostoks 3 and 4 had not harmed the cosmonauts. Understandably, they were excited and tired when they landed, but detailed examinations revealed them to be as healthy as ever.

Soviet government officials and scientists hailed the success of the first group flight. They predicted that cosmonauts would soon be going to the moon and to the planets.

Ten months passed before another Vostok roared into space from Tyuratam. When Moscow radio announced the launching on June 14, 1963, Vostok 5 was already completing its first orbit of the earth. The brief radio announcement supplied few details: The pilot was twenty-eight-year-old Valery Fyodorovich Bykovsky. He had successfully withstood the acceleration of lift-off and the transition to the zero gravity of orbital flight. The timing of the announcement and its brevity contrasted sharply with the full coverage the United States had given to the launching of Astronaut Gordon Cooper on a twenty-two-orbit flight a month earlier.

At the end of his second orbit of the earth, Cosmonaut Valery Bykovsky, using the call sign Hawk, radioed that he felt fine. The cosmonaut reported that all the systems of his spaceship were functioning smoothly.

The fifth Russian to go into space was a dark-haired young man who had been Andrian Nikolayev's backup pilot. The son of a transport worker, Bykovsky had grown up in a small town near Moscow. As a child he wanted to be a sailor. He joined the army, however, and entered pilot training. "He has always been courageous, and exciting and dangerous professions attracted him," his father said of Valery, who became a jet pilot in Russia's air defense forces. He also served as a parachute instructor.

Bykovsky began training for space flight with the first group of cosmonauts. He was popular with the other cosmonauts, who described him as "a jolly good fellow, the general favorite." He excelled at sports. His favorite game was *gorodki*, a form of bowling, but he also liked soccer, basketball, and hockey.

While Cosmonaut Bykovsky orbited the earth, Tass, the Soviet news agency, announced the official purpose of his mission. It was to continue the study of the effect of space flight on the human organism, to carry out research related to prolonged space flight, and to further test the Vostok spaceship. The Tass announcement said nothing of a second cosmonaut joining Bykovsky in space, but many people expected that to happen. Moreover, they thought that the second cosmonaut might be a woman. The Soviet Union had trained a class of women cosmonauts and the World Women's Congress was meeting in Moscow on June 24. It seemed like a perfect time to send a woman into space.

Alone in space for the time being, Cosmonaut Bykovsky carried out the day's tasks as listed in his flight program. It kept him busy until the end of Vostok 5's seventh orbit. It was shortly after midnight when he sent his final report to Ground Control. "All systems are working normally," he radioed. Then he went to sleep.

In the United States, TV viewers saw film of the cosmonaut in his spacecraft and shots of Muscovites lining up to buy newspapers that featured the flight of Vostok 5. The telecast came to the United States through a complicated hookup that began with

Intervision, the Eastern European TV system. In Helsinki, Finland, the broadcast was picked up by Western Europe's Eurovision system and transmitted to London. English technicians taped and edited the program before broadcasting it to the orbiting communications satellite, Telstar 2. A receiving station in Maine picked up Telstar's signals and fed the broadcast to American television networks. The Vostok 5 telecast was one of the few times that Telstar had been used as a television link between the Soviet Union and the United States.

Cosmonaut Bykovsky, now a seasoned space traveler, was crossing the Soviet Union on his thirty-first revolution when Vostok 6 joined Vostok 5 in orbit on June 16. In Moscow, loudspeakers boomed out to Sunday strollers: "A woman has gone into space!"

Vostok 6's pilot was Cosmonaut Valentina Tereshkova. From her spaceship she reported that she was feeling fine. The world's first spacewoman was a twenty-six-year-old former tire-factory and cotton-mill worker. Evening classes and trade school had enabled her to become a cotton spinning technologist in Yaroslavl, a town about 160 miles northeast of Moscow. Valentina, or Valya, as she was known to her friends, joined the Yaroslavl Aero Club and the parachuters' club at her factory. She became an accomplished parachutist, who regularly made difficult jumps.

Valentina learned about the Soviet Union's manned space program at the time of Cosmonaut Yuri Gagarin's pioneering one-orbit flight. Parachute training, she reasoned, should be as helpful to a cosmonaut as pilot training. She volunteered to become a cosmonaut and was accepted.

The fact that the Soviet Union had admitted a woman who wasn't a pilot to cosmonaut training surprised United States space officials. At that time all of NASA's astronauts were not only experienced flyers, but skillful test pilots as well. The Americans suggested that the Russians must have unlimited confidence in their automatic equipment. Or perhaps the Russians thought that any intelligent person could be trained to perform the tasks required of a cosmonaut.

Although NASA was considering the possibility of including scientists in its three-man Project Apollo crews, there were no plans to send a woman into space. Several women pilots had taken and passed the first phase of the physical and mental tests given to astronauts, but the use of women astronauts was "way down the road," as one NASA official put it.

Cosmonaut Valentina Tereshkova, pilot of Vostok 6, and Vostok 5's pilot, Valery Bykovsky. Cosmonaut Tereshkova became the first woman to fly in space, and later married Cosmonaut Andrian Nikolayev.

Valentina Tereshkova was one of a small class of women cosmonauts who began training in 1962. All were parachute jumpers and a few were pilots. Their training was similar to that of the male cosmonauts. In addition, those who could not already do so, learned to fly an airplane.

During their training, the spacewomen met Chief Designer Sergei Korolev, who pleased them by knowing all their names and backgrounds. He discussed the manned space program and showed them a Vostok.

Yuri Gagarin has written that it was sometimes difficult for Valentina to understand rocket technology and the more complicated spacecraft systems, but she overcame her difficulties by hard work. In June, 1963, she was named the pilot of Vostok 6.

With the other cosmonauts, Valentina Tereshkova watched the launching of Vostok 5 at Tyuratam. Two days later, dressed in an orange space suit with a white dove embroidered on the left breast, she went into space in Vostok 6, to join Vostok 5 in orbit.

Only 3 miles separated Vostok 5 and Vostok 6 at the beginning of their group flight. In a joint message the cosmonauts announced: "We are at a close distance from each other. All systems in the ships are working excellently. Feeling well."

Because Vostok 5's orbit ranged from 109 to 138 miles above the earth and Vostok 6's orbit varied from 114 to 145 miles, the distance between them grew greater with each circuit. The cosmonauts were able to maintain good radio communication, however, and messages flashed back and forth as they exchanged information about conditions aboard their Vostoks and relayed messages from the ground.

During Cosmonaut Tereshkova's first afternoon in space, she fell asleep and failed to answer a call from Ground Control. A worried Ground Control radioman contacted Cosmonaut Bykovsky for help. "Hawk, Hawk, this is Dawn [Ground Control]," he radioed. "Wake up Sea Gull [Cosmonaut Tereshkova]. She is probably asleep."

When Valentina spoke with Chief Designer Korolev that evening she told him: "I fell asleep for some time contrary to schedule. Excuse me. I shall do better. I feel fine."

In spite of the unscheduled nap, Soviet scientists expressed satisfaction with the performance of the first woman in space. Medical data relayed to the ground indicated that she was in a physiologically normal state, the scientists reported.

In one of several live broadcasts from space presented on Soviet TV, Valentina appeared stern as she concentrated on her work, but after listening to a radio message from the ground, she broke into a happy smile. The TV cameras caught Cosmonaut Bykovsky as he tried, and failed, to catch a drop of water that floated in his cabin. In some of his telecasts he gave cheerful thumbs-up signs to indicate that all was well.

The cosmonauts' schedules called for them to eat four times a day, although their mealtimes differed because of the difference in their launch times. In addition to food in tubes, each Vostok was supplied with meat pies, cutlets, fried veal, chicken fillets, beef tongue, minced meat, caviar sandwiches, oranges, lemons, apples, and candy. The food, cut into small pieces to make eating easier, was packed in plastic bags. Individual containers held enough bags to make a meal.

Drinking water for the cosmonauts was adapted to their individual tastes. If a cosmonaut requested it, water would even be brought from his home area. Inside the Vostok, water was stored in jars under heavy pressure. When a cosmonaut pressed a button, water flowed through a rubber tube to a mouthpiece.

For washing, the cosmonauts used pieces of cheesecloth presoaked with a cleansing liquid. Instead of attempting to brush their teeth in the gravity-free spaceship, they used a mouth rinse.

Early in the afternoon on June 18, Cosmonaut Valery Bykovsky broke the space record of 3 days 22 hours 22 minutes set by Cosmonaut Andrian Nikolayev. Bykovsky, now heavily bearded, showed no signs of fatigue in his TV appearances and he continued to report that all of his spacecraft's systems were functioning normally. Vostok 5 was beginning to lose altitude, however, and it appeared that the spaceship could remain in orbit only a few days more.

Although they did report that Vostok 5's orbit was getting progressively lower, Soviet authorities did not announce when the group flight would end. But it did end the next day. Vostok 6 came down first, after forty-eight orbits of the earth. Both Cosmonaut Tereshkova and the spacecraft landed safely under separate parachutes.

Workmen building a bridge near a village 380 miles northeast of the Kazakhstan coal-mining and industrial center of Karaganda were the first to spot Valentina's red and white parachute drifting to earth. The cosmonaut reported that the villagers welcomed her "in the Russian fashion with bread and salt." This was followed by a hearty meal while she awaited the arrival of the official recovery party. Although she looked tired after seventy hours and fifty minutes in space, the cosmonaut appeared to be in good health. "Only my nose is bruised," she said.

When Cosmonaut Bykovsky received orders to prepare for reentry, he radioed Ground Control: "I can go further. There is sufficient reserve of power, sufficient air and water. I am ready to continue the flight." But Ground Control told the reluctant cosmonaut to return to earth, and he did. In fifty-four minutes less than five full days in space he had completed eighty-one orbits of the earth and traveled 2,000,000 miles.

From his landing site in a field 330 miles northwest of Karaganda, the cosmonaut reported that he was unscratched and feeling fine. One of the farmers who helped the cosmonaut get out of his space suit told newsmen: "He looked a little tired, but his eyes were laughing."

The Soviet Union's newest pair of space travelers were re-

Moscow, June 22, 1963. Cosmonauts Tereshkova and Bykovsky receive a warm welcome at Vnukovo Airport after their successful flights.

united at a rest camp maintained for the cosmonauts. From there they went to Moscow for the traditional hero's welcome.

Soviet space officials announced that they were pleased with the results of the second group flight. In a communiqué they said: "New valuable data have been obtained about the influence of different factors of a space flight of long duration on the organisms of man and woman." The communiqué continued: "Rich factual material necessary for further perfection of the systems of piloted spaceships has been obtained."

At a press conference in Moscow, Cosmonaut Bykovsky stated that the group flight of Vostok 5 and Vostok 6 had been carried out exactly as planned. All of the tasks assigned to him and to Cosmonaut Tereshkova had been fulfilled, he said.

Some Western observers questioned the Soviet assessment of the dual space mission. They gave the Russians full credit for what was accomplished, but they wondered if something more had not been planned for Vostok 5 and Vostok 6. Unlike earlier Soviet space missions, each one of which had achieved something new, the second group flight represented no great advance over the flight of Vostok 3 and Vostok 4.

Had the Russians planned to link the two spaceships? Their orbits were too far apart to do that without a great deal of maneuvering in space. Perhaps a third capsule was involved, one whose orbit would have been closer to that of Vostok 5 if it could have been launched. Or perhaps Vostok 5 itself had not been launched into an orbit precise enough to make a linkup with another ship possible. And even Vostok 5's record five-day flight fell short of the eight days that experts had predicted for it.

No further explanation was forthcoming from Soviet authorities. A few months later they did make an announcement about Vostok 6's pilot, Cosmonaut Valentina Tereshkova. She was going to marry a fellow cosmonaut, Vostok 3 pilot Andrian Nikolayev. The wedding took place on November 3, 1963.

6 | THE VOSKHOD REPLACES THE VOSTOK

If the group flight of Vostok 5 and Vostok 6 seemed to be a repeat of the previous Soviet space effort, the next mission to leave Tyuratam was a different one indeed. On October 12, 1964, three cosmonauts were launched into earth orbit in a new spaceship called Voskhod, or Sunrise. Moreover, only the spacecraft commander was a trained pilot. One of his companions was a designer-scientist, the other was a physician.

Voskhod 1's commander was thirty-seven-year-old Vladimir Mikhailovich Komarov, a former jet pilot. A native of Moscow, Komarov began air force training at fifteen. He served as a fighter pilot before attending the Zhukovsky Air Force Engineering Academy in Moscow, an advanced technical school similar to the United States Air Force's Institute of Technology at Wright-Patterson Air Force Base, Ohio. Before he was chosen as a cosmonaut, Komarov was assigned to the Soviet Air Force Research Institute.

Vladimir Komarov almost failed to complete cosmonaut training when hospitalization and an operation raised grave doubts about his ability to continue the strenuous program. He was able, however, to convince the doctors that he could keep up, and he did so well that he was chosen as the backup pilot for the Vostok 4 mission. But more troubles lay ahead. During one of the cosmonaut's training rides in a centrifuge, the doctors discovered that he had developed a systolic heart murmur. Once again they questioned his fitness for space flight. With the help of several heart specialists who certified that his condition was not dangerous, Komarov was readmitted to the cosmonaut program. His selection to command Voskhod 1 followed.

Konstantin Petrovich Feoktistov, Voskhod 1's scientist-cosmonaut, served in the Russian army during World War II. After the war he completed his education, graduating from the Bauman Higher Technical College, one of the Soviet Union's best engineering schools.

Before he began training for the Voskhod 1 flight, the blond,

Cosmonaut Vladimir Komarov, Voskhod 1 commander.

thirty-eight-year-old Feoktistov worked on spaceship design. He also gave lectures to the cosmonauts on spaceship engineering.

Voskhod 1's third crew member was a specialist in aviation and space medicine. The son of one of the Soviet Union's leading brain surgeons, Boris Borisovich Yegorov grew up in Moscow and attended medical school there. After graduation, the young doctor did research in aviation and space medicine, specializing in the vestibular apparatus of the inner ear.

For Cosmonauts Feoktistov and Yegorov, preparation for the

Soviet Cosmonaut Konstantin Feoktistov, a research scientist, was a crew member of Voskhod 1.

flight of Voskhod 1 included training in simulators and in a centrifuge. They also experienced the condition of weightlessness by taking special plane rides. According to Voskhod 1's commander: "They went through all the sections of the training program that are necessary for a twenty-four-hour flight."

For the Soviet Union's first multi-man spaceship, Chief Designer Sergei Korolev had developed a larger capsule and a more powerful booster to lift it into orbit. The capsule, which was round,

Soviet Cosmonaut Boris Yegorov, a physician.

weighed 11,730 pounds. Antennas and a parachute canister were located at the top, and retro-rockets protruded from the bottom.

Inside, the roomy and comfortable Voskhod was padded with a white material that acted as soundproofing. Three contour seats stood in a row before the instrument panel, which was larger than the Vostok's, although many of the instruments were the same. Each cosmonaut had his own viewport. Lockers held food, water, warm clothing, and life jackets, the latter for use in case of a landing on water.

Voskhod's booster, described as a "powerful new launch vehicle," had seven engines with a total thrust of 1,433,000 pounds. The Vostok's six engines had delivered 1,323,000 pounds of thrust.

Like the cosmonauts who had flown in the Vostoks, Voskhod 1's crew spent the night before their launching in the cosmonauts' cottage at Tyuratam. After dinner they reviewed the flight schedule one more time and worked on their logbooks. They also played host to a group of their fellow cosmonauts, including Yuri Gagarin. Although they joked and laughed, the visitors were all a little anxious about the next day's flight, "more worried than we ourselves," Vladimir Komarov observed later.

Before long an imposing figure appeared at the door of the cosmonauts' quarters. It was Chief Designer Korolev, who had heard the noise they were making. "I knew there'd be bedlam here," he said. "Let the boys rest before the flight."

When the three cosmonauts arrived at the launching pad the next morning, they wore light woolen suits and blue zippered jackets. The Chief Designer had decided that bulky space suits were not necessary in the Voskhod. The spacecraft's efficient air system provided its passengers with a mixture of gases to breathe that was fairly close to that found in the earth's atmosphere at a pressure slightly higher than the normal 14.7 pounds per square inch at sea level. Temperature and humidity were both controlled. If a meteoroid were to puncture the Voskhod's skin in the vacuum of space, the cosmonauts would be in trouble without pressure suits and helmets, but the Chief Designer did not expect that to happen.

Before entering the Voskhod, the cosmonauts took off their shoes and put on light flight boots. Dr. Yegorov was the first to take his seat, then Cosmonaut Feoktistov entered the Voskhod followed by Spacecraft Commander Komarov. The cosmonauts were pleased with the Voskhod's contour seats. "There was even a depression for my head," Komarov observed.

The spacemen had little time to relax, however. Their duties began at once. The doctor checked pulses and found them normal. His companions tested equipment and made entries in the logbooks. Messages were exchanged with the control center until a controller announced "Ignition!" and "Start!"

Commander Komarov later wrote of the launching: "We were expecting some extraordinary sensation. But there was nothing special. The rocket shivered a bit, there was a slight noise."

Voskhod 1's upward movement produced only a small increase in g-forces. "It was much easier than on the centrifuge," Komarov reported. He was able to talk with his fellow cosmonauts and the controllers, make an entry in his logbook, and observe the steppes and forests beneath him. Soon he was radioing: "Have reached orbit. All is normal."

As it moved around the earth, Voskhod 1's orbit varied in altitude from 100 to 255 miles. It was traveling both lower and higher than the Vostoks had. Inside the orbiting spacecraft, the cosmonauts were busy carrying out their assigned tasks.

Perhaps Dr. Yegorov was the busiest of the three. He was the first doctor to conduct tests in space and there were many things he wanted to learn. His equipment included devices for measuring heart action, lung action, and brain waves. With a device called a dynamometer, he tested the strength of the cosmonauts' hands to determine when they began to tire. Another device measured the light sensitivity of their eyes. He took numerous blood samples that were later analyzed to see if any changes occurred as the flight progressed.

Dr. Yegorov was especially interested in studying the relationship between the sense of balance and weightlessness. In one of his investigations, he periodically asked his fellow cosmonauts to rotate their heads ten times while they were hooked up to instruments that measured their reactions. Beginning with Voskhod 1's second orbit, the doctor had a personal case of disorientation to study. He began to feel as if he were flying through space upside down. Gherman Titov had experienced the same sensation at the beginning of his Vostok 2 flight. Fortunately, Yegorov's disorientation was not severe and he was able to continue with his investigations.

Writing later of his experiences in space, Dr. Yegorov described the convenience of working in a weightless environment: "For instance, when working with several instruments, one of them has to be laid somewhere for several seconds. But you don't have to think of a place for it during weightlessness. It doesn't have to be put under oneself or on the floor. You simply hang it in the air a bit to the side, and again take it when it is needed. It doesn't get lost anywhere. That's very convenient."

Every ninety minutes, as Voskhod 1 crossed the Soviet Union, the cosmonauts appeared on television. A few of the telecasts were blurred, but often viewers could clearly identify the spacemen. During one telecast, when an announcer asked the rather serious-looking Konstantin Feoktistov to smile, he replied with a wide grin.

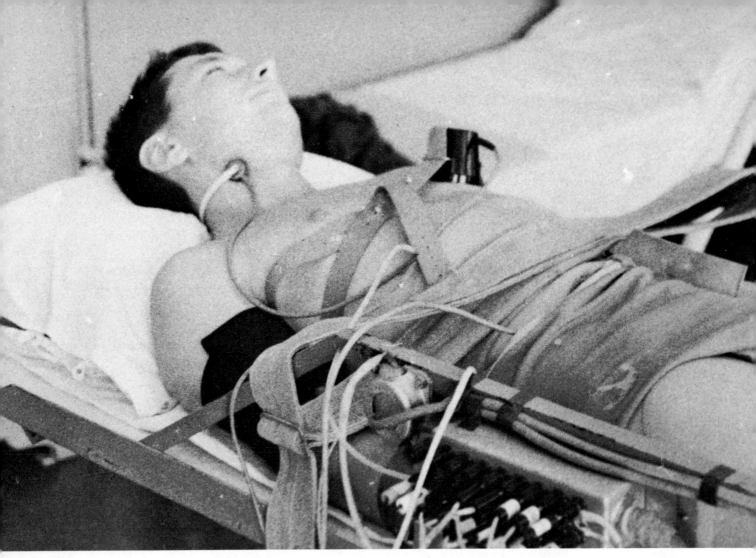

Dr. Boris Yegorov, the physician-cosmonaut, is shown here undergoing a medical checkup.

In addition to the programs from space, Soviet television showed numerous still and moving pictures of the cosmonauts that had been taken when they were in training or with their families.

Voskhod 1 was over the North Pole when the cosmonauts noticed a flickering light in their cabin. Konstantin Feoktistov identified the source as a luminous phenomenon of the polar regions called aurora borealis in the Northern Hemisphere and aurora australis in the Southern. Through a porthole they observed radiant yellowish-white columns of various sizes massed on the horizon, something none of the space travelers before them had seen. All three crew members wrote descriptions of the aurora borealis in their logbooks.

During his space flight, American Astronaut John Glenn had

reported seeing mysterious luminous particles around his orbiting craft. The Voskhod 1 crew saw similar particles floating near their ship. Cosmonaut Komarov described them as sparkling "like little beams from a pencil of light cast upon an emerald." The cosmonauts decided that they were probably dust particles that had traveled into space with Voskhod 1.

The three men saw many things that fascinated them. In their logbooks and on tape they described the moon and the stars as they appeared against the blackness of space, lightning flaring from clouds over Africa, icebergs that looked like "crumbs" in the ocean near Antarctica, the long, snow-covered ranges of the Himalayas, and other wonders of space and the earth below.

With so much to observe, Voskhod 1's crew would have liked to greatly reduce, or even eliminate, the time set aside for eating and sleeping. But they had a schedule to follow and at the prescribed hour they got out packages of food. At dinner the cosmonauts discovered that they could send packages of meat pie and tubes of juice floating back and forth in a kind of "air delivery" system. Their appetites were good, "just like on earth," the spaceship commander reported. They also slept well, untroubled by the fact that their arms, unconfined by straps, rose toward the ceiling.

Although Soviet space officials had announced that the principal assignment of the Voskhod 1 crew was to study the working capacity of a group during a long flight, the spacecraft was scheduled to return to earth after twenty-four hours. The cosmonauts were reluctant to terminate their mission, however. When he received the order to prepare for a landing, Spacecraft Commander Komarov radioed: "We have seen so much that is interesting. We would like to clarify some things and to understand them even better. The crew requests to continue the flight for another twenty-four hours."

Chief Designer Sergei Korolev replied with a Russian version of a line from Shakespeare: "There are many, oh friend Horatio, wonders in the earth," adding, "of course, there is a lot that is interesting, but we shall stay within the program."

Accordingly, the well-disciplined cosmonauts began at once to stow away all the loose objects in their spacecraft. A piece of equipment flying through the cabin during the deceleration of re-entry into the earth's atmosphere could cause serious injury.

Voskhod 1's descent from space began with the firing of the craft's retro-rockets when it was over Africa at the end of the sixteenth orbit. As the ship entered the earth's atmosphere, the cosmonauts watched a pale pink glow outside their portholes turn orange, then red. Voskhod 1's heat shield reached a temperature of 10,000 degrees Fahrenheit, but the men inside remained comfortable. However, they did feel the increasing pressure of deceleration and a vibration that they compared to driving a car over cobblestones. Meanwhile, the earth was getting closer.

Voskhod 1's crew was scheduled to land in the spaceship. To achieve a "soft" landing, Chief Designer Korolev had developed a set of braking rockets that operated near the ground to lower the craft to a gentle touchdown after a huge parachute had slowed its rate of descent. Unlike the Vostok spacecraft, Voskhod 1 had no device for ejecting the cosmonauts before the landing.

American astronauts have always come down on water, which allows a softer landing than hard ground. A retro-rocket braking system, similar to the one developed for the Voskhod, was not used on American capsules because it would have added too much weight.

Although they were prepared for a decided bump when Voskhod 1 touched down, the cosmonauts felt nothing. "There was a rustle under us and a scratching against sand," Komarov recalled. In fact, Feoktistov described it as a "feather-bed landing." Voskhod 1 had come down in a field in the Kazakhstan recovery area, about 350 miles northeast of Tyuratam.

Farm workers rushed to greet the cosmonauts when they emerged from their spaceship into the cold morning air. Soon search planes appeared. The first pilot to spot the Voskhod 1 spacecraft radioed: "The object is visible on the ground, well visible, and the cosmonauts, three, beside it. They're walking about, walking briskly. Congratulations to all, to all!"

At Kustanaya, the town nearest to the landing site, the residents greeted the returned spacemen with handshakes, flowers, and speeches. The cosmonauts, wearing athletes' sweat suits, looked tired but happy as they began the postflight activities that culminated in a great victory parade in Moscow's Red Square.

In speeches and articles, Soviet officials praised the first multimanned space flight. They indicated that it was a step toward the construction of a space platform that could be used for future missions to the moon and the planets.

Five months later, another Voskhod left the Tyuratam launching pad. Outwardly it resembled Voskhod 1, but Chief Designer Korolev had made an important interior change. Instead of a third crew seat, Voskhod 2 had an air-lock chamber that would enable a cosmonaut to leave the craft in space.

Because nitrogen was one of the components of the Voskhod's air system, a cosmonaut wearing a pressure suit could not simply depressurize the capsule, open a hatch, and step out into the vacuum of space. The United States Project Gemini, whose capsules contained only oxygen, was planning to use such a method. But if a cosmonaut did that he would develop a disease called the bends, as nitrogen bubbles formed in his body tissues. In Korolev's air-lock chamber a cosmonaut could breathe enough pure oxygen to wash the nitrogen out of his system. Then it would be safe for him to leave the Voskhod.

Chief Designer Korolev favored an air system containing nitrogen as well as oxygen for his capsules because it greatly reduced the danger of fire. Moreover, he was planning for the day when cosmonauts would be assembling space stations and performing other tasks outside their craft. If they could leave through an air-lock chamber, the entire ship would not have to be depressurized and the cosmonauts who remained inside would not have to wear bulky pressure suits.

Soviet space officials chose the first cosmonaut to use Korolev's air-lock chamber with great care. They picked Alexei Ark-

Cosmonaut Alexei Leonov.

hipovich Leonov, a thirty-year-old former air force flyer and an amateur artist. He has been described as a man of endurance, cold-bloodedness, high discipline, and magnificent physical development.

Leonov was born in the coal-mining region of Siberia, the second youngest of nine children. As a younger man he had attended aviation school and had become a fighter pilot. He was also a skillful parachutist, attaining the rank of parachute instructor.

During the search for cosmonauts in the late 1950's, the examining board told Alexei Leonov that he was under consideration for "something new, something very, very difficult." The prospect appealed to the adventurous Alexei who was chosen with the first group of cosmonauts. During his training, he took and passed numerous psychological tests to make sure he would react favorably to being alone outside a spacecraft.

Oil painting and pencil sketching were Leonov's hobbies. He told his fellow cosmonauts that he would like to take oil paints, or at least colored pencils, into orbit with him. While he waited for his space assignment, Leonov served as editor and illustrator of the one-page cosmonaut newspaper, *Neptune*.

The man selected as Voskhod 2's commander was Pavel Ivanovich Belyayev, who, at thirty-nine, was one of the oldest of the cosmonauts. He had grown up in the northern part of European Russia, where he became an expert skier. In the winter, the future cosmonaut had been used to skiing 3 miles to school. His favorite subjects were physics and geography.

During World War II, Belyayev trained as a fighter pilot. When he was graduated at the end of the war, he had reported for flying duty with the Russian navy in the Far East and remained there for eleven years.

Belyayev was attending the Soviet Air Force Academy when he became a candidate for the cosmonaut corps. He easily passed the entrance tests and amazed examiners with his ability to endure long rides on the centrifuge.

As had Cosmonaut Vladimir Komarov, Pavel Belyayev had difficulty completing the cosmonaut training program. His problem was a double fracture of the left leg just above the ankle, which he had incurred during a parachute jump. The fracture healed very slowly and Belyayev was in danger of being eliminated until he began exercising with increasingly heavy dumbbells. This weight-lifting therapy worked. The cosmonaut had been able to resume training after he made another parachute jump to prove that the accident had not made him afraid of jumping.

Cosmonaut Pavel Belyayev.

Veteran Voskhod pilots Vladimir Komarov, Konstantin Feoktistov, and Boris Yegorov helped Leonov and Belyayev prepare for their important space mission. With Komarov, they practiced flight procedures in simulators and in the Voskhod 2 spacecraft where they worked with the new air-lock chamber. Feoktistov helped them with camera techniques and navigation problems. Dr. Yegorov taught them how to carry out inflight medical tests.

On March 18, 1965, the day of the Voskhod 2 launching, late winter snow covered the ground at Tyuratam. After the usual pre-launch ceremony, Cosmonauts Belyayev and Leonov rode the elevator to the waiting spaceship. Voskhod 2's dials glowed softly as they settled into their seats. Overhead, within easy reach of both men, was the instrument panel for the new air-lock chamber. Another set of controls had been installed within the chamber itself. The main instrument panel was located above Belyayev's position. The black handle for manually controlling the ship was at his side. Television cameras looked down from the ceiling. A camera was also mounted inside the air-lock chamber and another had been installed outside the chamber's exit into space.

Voskhod 2 lifted off the launching pad at 10:00 A.M., Moscow time, and went into an orbit that the Russians announced was "close to the prescribed one." It carried the spaceship 308 miles from the earth at its farthest point and 107 miles at its closest.

As soon as Voskhod 2 was safely in orbit, the cosmonauts began preparations for Alexei Leonov's "space walk." With Belyayev's help, Leonov put on a haversack-type life-support unit over his pressure suit and began breathing its oxygen. His suit was a special garment designed to protect the cosmonaut from the vacuum, temperature extremes, radiation, and other hazards of space. With it he wore a white metal helmet that had a dark visor-filter, gloves, and specially designed boots.

After Leonov moved through a hatch into the air-lock chamber, he pressurized his suit and checked to make sure that it was airtight and that the helmet was adjusted properly. Then he signaled Belyayev to close the hatch. While he waited for Belyayev to depressurize the sealed chamber, Leonov reviewed the procedures for stepping out into space. He was eager to be on his way. Finally the outer hatch door opened. "I was struck by a flow of blindingly bright sunlight, like an arc of electric welding," Leonov later recalled.

After a preliminary look out of the hatch, Leonov told the spaceship commander over the intercom: "I'm pushing off."

"Wait a minute," Pavel Belyayev cautioned, "don't be in a hurry."

Standing in the hatch opening, Leonov waited while Belyayev checked his pulse and respiration readings and the readings from the life-support system. Satisfied that everything was operating normally, Belyayev gave the order to leave.

"When I was ready to go, I gave a little push and popped out of the hatch like a cork," Leonov recalled.

Voskhod 2 was over the Soviet Union at the beginning of its second orbit when the cosmonaut left the spacecraft. Although he had heard many accounts of what space looked like, he was surprised at what he now saw. "Ahead of me was black sky, very black," Leonov said later. "The sun was not radiant, just a smooth disk without an aureole. Below was the smooth, level earth. You could not tell it was a sphere, except from the fact that the round edge showed on the horizon."

The space walker remained attached to the Voskhod by a 5-yard lifeline that enclosed a telephone cable and telemetric wires. Oxygen was supplied by the life-support unit on the cosmonaut's back.

One of Leonov's first jobs outside the spacecraft was to remove the lens cap from the camera that would record his activities. As he held the cap in his gloved hand he considered launching it into an orbit of its own. "But I decided not to litter space," he recalled. "So I threw it with all my strength toward the earth, looking after it until it disappeared from view."

When the space walker pushed off from the Voskhod, the ship seemed to lurch forward. Inside the capsule, Cosmonaut Belyayev felt this accelerated movement. "I could hear him knock on the cabin wall with a boot," the commander recalled. "I even heard him move his hands over the ship's surface."

Meanwhile, the TV camera was following the space walker's movements. Viewers in the Soviet Union and Europe saw him float away from the Voskhod with his legs outstretched. Then he slowly turned a somersault, rolled over several times, and finally stood on his head. Behind the cosmonaut, the earth was moving from right to left.

At a distance of about 15 feet from the spacecraft, Leonov admired the Voskhod. "It floated majestically," he said, almost solemnly. "It looked mysterious, fantastic. The portholes seemed like big eyes, the antennas like tentacles. All you needed was electronic music."

Armed with a movie camera, the cosmonaut took pictures of the Voskhod. He and the vehicle were both racing through space at a speed of nearly 5 miles per second, but Leonov did not feel as if he was traveling that fast. Rather, he described his movements as "swimming in space," or "floating." When his lifeline was stretched to its full length, the cosmonaut began to rotate. This rotation continued until it was stopped by the increased twisting of the tether.

Leonov returned to the Voskhod by simply pulling on his lifeline. A strong tug brought the ship rapidly toward him. "I had to ward it off with my arms to avoid breaking the visor of my helmet," he recalled.

Leonov's efforts in space, which included dismantling a camera and removing several objects from the outside of the capsule, had tired him. It was difficult to move in the bulky pressure suit in spite of the bellows-like devices that helped him to bend his torso, arms, and legs. When neatly winding up the lifeline on his hand — as he was supposed to — proved troublesome, the cosmonaut simply pushed it through the hatch door. Then he went through the door himself. He had been outside the capsule for ten minutes and, counting the time spent in the depressurized air-lock chamber, in the vacuum of space a total of twenty minutes.

Spacecraft Commander Belyayev had been using television to keep a sharp eye on his fellow cosmonaut. In addition, he had closely monitored the operation of Leonov's life-support system and his pulse and respiration rates. Now he quickly closed the hatch door and raised the pressure in the air-lock chamber. "Good for you!" he complimented the space walker.

When Leonov returned to his seat in Voskhod 2, streams of perspiration were running down his face. Nevertheless, he went to work on his logbook after only a short rest, and for ninety minutes recorded his impressions of the space walk.

Meanwhile, the flight of Voskhod 2 continued, with the spacecraft circling the earth once every ninety minutes. The busy cosmonauts had dials and gauges to watch and experiments to conduct. They took both still and motion pictures of the marvelous sights of space. They were unable to photograph one of the phenomena they witnessed, however. It was another artificial satellite that appeared briefly near Voskhod 2. "We shouted with surprise when we saw it slowly rotating about 800 meters [900 yards] from our ship," Belyayev recalled.

At that time, both the United States and the Soviet Union had unmanned satellites orbiting the earth, but the cosmonauts were unable to identify the one they saw. United States experts speculated that it was probably a Russian satellite, since it must have been launched originally on a path somewhat similar to that of Voskhod 2.

During their seventh orbit, the cosmonauts appeared in a live telecast that showed them strapped to their seats in a brightly sun-lit cabin. Later, the cosmonauts took turns sleeping while an official announcement assured the world that both men were feeling well and all spacecraft systems were functioning normally.

Voskhod 2 Cosmonaut Leonov during his "space walk" in March, 1965.

Voskhod 2 was scheduled to land during its seventeenth orbit. For more than twenty-four hours the craft had performed flawlessly. During landing preparations, however, it became apparent that the automatic solar orientation system was not working properly. This was a device that should have placed Voskhod 2 in the correct position for reentry by "locking" onto the sun. Then, when braking rockets were fired, the craft would leave its orbit and head directly for the landing area in Kazakhstan.

Commander Belyayev and Ground Control discussed Voskhod 2's problem. The cosmonaut requested permission to take over from the automatic system and land the spaceship manually. "The thirty seconds that elapsed while a decision was being made seemed very long," he recalled. "Finally we got the signal for manual descent in the eighteenth orbit."

All of the necessary calculations for a manually controlled landing had already been worked out. Using these, the cosmonauts maneuvered Voshkod 2 into the correct position and fired the braking rockets. The 13,000-pound craft left orbit and headed earthward. Its great speed as it pushed through the thickening atmosphere generated so much heat that the cosmonauts actually saw molten metal running down the portholes.

Voskhod 2 overshot the Kazakhstan landing area by 500 miles. It came down in a remote, snow-covered forest area that the Russians call *taiga*, some 750 miles northeast of Moscow. The nearest large town was Perm on the eastern slopes of the Ural Mountains.

Fortunately, the spacecraft landed between two trees in the thick forest. When the cosmonauts opened the hatch they were grateful for their arctic survival training. Deep snow lay all around them and it was very cold. They radioed that they had made a safe landing, but it was two days before they could be airlifted to Perm. Meanwhile, they huddled over a fire and tried to keep warm.

Cosmonauts Leonov and Belyayev being welcomed at Perm airport after their Voskhod 2 mission.

Cosmonaut Leonov and a Soviet artist combined their talents in this conception of a space station. The circular station, being constructed from large-diameter pipe sections, would be set in rotary motion, thus creating artificial gravity to combat the harmful effect of weightlessness.

Search planes dropped heavier clothing and additional survival gear and a doctor arrived with a ground rescue party. The physician insisted that the nearly frozen cosmonauts take a snow bath to prevent frostbite. After the initial chill, they felt warmer.

The returned space travelers left their landing site on skis. With the rescue party, they skied through 12 miles of steep, forested slopes to a clearing where lumberjacks had cut down enough trees to make a small helicopter landing pad. From there they flew to Perm in a long-range helicopter.

Several hundred people were on hand to greet the cosmonauts at the Perm airport. When newsmen asked Alexei Leonov how it felt to step out into space he told them: "I didn't experience any fear, only a sense of infinite expanse." He added: "I knew I wouldn't meet anyone I knew up there."

After a short stay at Perm, the cosmonauts flew back to Tyuratam. The undamaged Voskhod 2 was also airlifted back to the cosmodrome.

Voskhod 2's space walk added another important "first" to the Soviet Union's achievements, and Russian space officials hinted at more to come. Noting that Cosmonaut Leonov had demonstrated that men could work in space, one official predicted: "We shall yet live to see the day when orbiting platforms appear in space, resembling scientific research institutes in the earth's upper atmosphere." And another said: "The target now before us is the moon, and we hope to reach it in the not too distant future."

There was no formal announcement about a program for launching space laboratories or for reaching the moon, however. The world was left to wonder whether or not the Soviet Union planned to concentrate on space laboratories. Or did that country hope to best the United States's announced goal of landing astronauts on the moon by 1970?

7 | FAILURE AND SUCCESS AT TYURATAM

Four days after Voskhod 2 landed, the United States launched Gemini 3. It was the first manned mission of Project Gemini, a space program designed to develop the techniques that would be needed for landing astronauts on the moon. Gemini 4, which featured a 21-minute space walk by Astronaut Edward White, followed in June.

During the next seventeen months, there were eight more Gemini missions, and one of them, Gemini 7, lasted for a record 330 hours and 35 minutes. Gemini 6, launched eleven days after Gemini 7, rendezvoused within one foot of the latter craft. Gemini 8 accomplished the first successful docking in space when it linked up with an orbiting Agena rocket. During the other Gemini missions, astronauts practiced rendezvous, docking, and extravehicular activity (EVA), all vital to the success of the United States plan for reaching and exploring the moon.

While the American astronauts were busy in space with their Gemini missions, the Soviet Union's cosmonauts remained on the ground. Western observers began to wonder if there really was a race between the United States and the Soviet Union to reach the moon first. Perhaps the Russians had given up any plans they might have had for such a project. The United States, on the other hand, moved rapidly ahead with its Project Apollo moon-landing program.

The National Aeronautics and Space Administration launched three unmanned Apollo spacecraft in 1966. By January, 1967, preparations were under way for the first manned Apollo mission when disaster struck in the form of a fire that destroyed an Apollo spacecraft and killed Astronauts Virgil Grissom, Edward White, and Roger Chaffee. While NASA investigated the cause of the fire and took corrective measures, Project Apollo missions were suspended.

Although no cosmonauts went into space after the Voskhod 2 flight, the Russians did launch several unmanned craft. Some traveled to the moon; others went into earth orbit carrying a variety of scientific and military payloads. On the basis of what they could learn about this activity, Western observers concluded that the Soviets did not have a moon-landing program similar to the United States Project Apollo. However, there were rumors that the secretive Russians were working on a new craft to replace the Voskhod for manned space flight, perhaps for a flight to the moon.

One of the reasons for the delay in the appearance of the new Soviet spacecraft might have been the death of Chief Designer Sergei Korolev in January, 1966. In keeping with Soviet policy, the name of Korolev's successor was not announced, but he was thought to be an engineer named Mikhail K. Yangel. Finishing the new spacecraft was one of the new Chief Designer's high-priority projects.

In 1966 and early 1967 the Soviets launched a number of Cosmos spacecraft into earth orbits. Since the name Cosmos was applied to a variety of unmanned spacecraft, Western observers could never be sure of their purpose. However, the orbital path of some of the satellites was similar to that used for manned flights. Moreover, they remained aloft only a few days, which was usually the case with practice launchings for manned missions. It seemed likely that the Russians were getting ready to put their new manned spacecraft into orbit.

The official announcement of the launching came on April 23, 1967. The unusually brief bulletin stated that a new piloted space-ship named Soyuz (pronounced Suh-yoosh, the name means Union) had gone into orbit at 3:55 A.M., Moscow time. Veteran spaceman Vladimir Komarov was at the controls.

Later it was announced that the purpose of the Soyuz 1 flight was to test the new spacecraft, carry out expanded scientific, physical, and technical experiments, and to further study the effect of space flight on the human organism. Russian citizens were assured that Cosmonaut Komarov was in good health, with a pulse rate of 82 a minute and a breathing rate of 20. Soyuz 1 was traveling at a speed of 18,640 miles an hour. The craft circled the earth every 88.6 minutes on an orbital path that ranged from 125 to about 140 miles above the earth. Radio communications with the spacecraft were good.

Tall, dark-haired Cosmonaut Komarov, who had commanded the three-man Voskhod 1 mission and helped train the Voskhod 2 pilots, was one of the most skilled of the cosmonauts. According to Tass, he was noted in the cosmonaut corps for his knowledge of engineering and his terrific capacity for work.

This still from a Soviet film pictures a Soyuz spacecraft just prior to blast-off.

Although the announced purpose of the Soyuz 1 flight contained nothing unusual, some observers suggested that Cosmonaut Komarov's launching could be the first step in a spectacular space mission. Perhaps a second craft carrying as many as five cosmonauts would join Soyuz 1 in orbit. Eventually, according to this theory, the Russians would link two of their new spaceships to form a manned orbiting laboratory.

An article by Cosmonaut Yuri Gagarin in a Russian magazine encouraged such speculation. In the article the cosmonaut implied that the Soviet Union was planning to send up a large space station. The time was not far off according to Gagarin. The station would remain in orbit for a long time and receive supplies from spacecraft shuttling from the earth.

It was also suggested that a Soyuz might be sent around the moon and back to earth. And there were reports that the new spacecraft weighed as much as 32 tons.

More than a year passed after the launching of Soyuz 1 before information about the spacecraft became available. Then drawings and descriptions in Russian newspapers indicated that it was divided into two separate spherical crew cabins and a compartment in the rear that housed temperature control equipment, a computer, power supplies, radio apparatus, and two large rocket engines and their fuel. One engine was a backup for the other.

During the critical periods of flight, such as launching, return to earth, and rendezvous with another spaceship, cosmonauts were to occupy the middle, or command, cabin, which was the safest. It was protected by heat shielding and contained most of the Soyuz's navigation instruments and the controls for the craft's maneuvering rockets. The compartment had two windows.

During most of their time in space, the cosmonauts would use the larger orbital compartment in the ship's forward end. It was reached by opening a hatch and climbing through a passageway. The forward cabin had facilities for eating, sleeping, exercising, and conducting scientific experiments. It had four windows.

The 13,000-pound Soyuz's 318 cubic feet of crew space gave the cosmonauts room to move about. By contrast, the single Apollo crew cabin contained only 210 cubic feet. The Soyuz could carry enough supplies to last one man for thirty days, or three men for ten days.

The Soyuz was cylindrical in shape. Two large, wing-like solar panels jutted from the midsection of the craft. Carrying solar cells to convert the energy of light into electrical energy, they deployed after the craft was in orbit to serve as a source of additional power for its instruments. Communications and radar antennas extended from the Soyuz's forward section.

Only the middle compartment of the Soyuz returned to earth after a space flight. When the time came to leave orbit, one of the engines in the rear compartment fired to slow the craft. Then the rear and forward compartments separated from the middle compartment that housed the cosmonauts. The middle compartment was equipped with small rockets to control the early part of the descent and braking rockets to slow the capsule when it neared the ground.

Cosmonaut Komarov, who had studied aeronautical engineering, was pleased that he had been chosen to pilot the Soviet Union's new spacecraft. "This ship is a major creative achievement of our designers, scientists, engineers, and workers," he said before the Soyuz 1 launching. "I am proud that I was given the right to test it in flight."

From space, the cosmonaut reported that his test flight was proceeding according to plan. He was in good health and feeling well. "Everything is all right," he radioed. The orbiting cosmonaut sent greetings to his fellow citizens, but there were no live television broadcasts from Soyuz 1.

Between 1:30 and 9:30 P.M., Moscow time, while the spaceship was orbiting too far from the Soviet Union for radio contact, the cosmonaut rested. Shortly after midnight, Tass announced that Soyuz 1 had completed thirteen orbits. In a 6:12 A.M. news release, Tass said: "According to the report of the pilot-cosmonaut Komarov and telemetered information, he is in good health and feels well. The ship's systems are functioning normally."

At the time of the news release the cosmonaut was preparing to return to earth after what appeared to be a successful seventeen-orbit test flight of the Soyuz. The spaceship was over Africa and heading for the Soviet Union when its retro-rockets fired to slow it down for reentry into the atmosphere. A Soviet newsman who was at Tyuratam reported that a ground controller radioed: "Well done!" when Komarov relayed the information that the retro-rocket system had functioned perfectly.

"Everything is working fine," Komarov repeated as the Soyuz began to lose altitude. "Everything is working perfectly."

According to the newsman, that was the last message received from Cosmonaut Komarov.

Apparently Soyuz 1 continued its descent to 23,000 feet. At that height, the craft's main parachute should have opened to slow its downward movement. But the parachute's lines became tangled and it did not fully deploy. Without the drag from the parachute, the Soyuz fell to the earth at great speed, carrying Cosmonaut Vladimir Komarov to his death.

Soviet and American space experts agree that reentry into the earth's atmosphere is one of the most critical maneuvers in a space flight. Computers must make rapid calculations to determine the precise moment when braking rockets are to be fired and the exact length of time they should burn. The rockets must perform flawlessly. A mistake or a malfunction could send a spaceship into a new orbit instead of back to earth. Or the craft could be sent earthward at too steep an angle, causing it to burn up as it rushed through the thickening atmosphere. Even a very slight error would make a spaceship miss its designated landing area. Whether a spaceship was designed to touch down on land, like the Vostoks, Voskhods, and the Soyuz, or on water, like United States spacecraft, parachutes were necessary to brake its fall. The fate of Soyuz 1 demonstrated just how important parachutes were to a safe landing.

As far as is known, Soyuz 1 did not have an ejection-seat system similar to the one built into the Vostoks to allow the cosmonauts to land separately from their craft. Furthermore, Komarov was evidently wearing neither a pressure suit nor a flying suit. He was reported to have boarded the Soyuz wearing a bright blue pullover, slacks, and light shoes.

When several hours passed with no news from Soyuz 1, rumors circulated in Moscow that the flight had run into trouble. Nevertheless, the Soviet people were stunned when they heard the official announcement that Cosmonaut Komarov had been killed.

The Soviet Union and the United States had launched a combined total of twenty-two manned orbital flights in which thirty-five cosmonauts and astronauts had spent twenty-five hundred hours in space. Komarov's death was the first to occur during a mission.

On the day following the fatal crash, an estimated 150,000 Russians waited in line to file past Cosmonaut Vladimir Komarov's flower-covered bier on the second floor of the House of the Soviet Army in Moscow. An honor guard of soldiers watched over the bier. Premier Alexei N. Kosygin, who had succeeded Nikita Khrushchev, joined them briefly, along with Soviet President Nikolai Podgorny. More soldiers stood at attention in the corridors and on the stairway under black-draped chandeliers.

On the succeeding day the flower-covered urn containing Cosmonaut Komarov's ashes was buried in the Kremlin wall, an honor reserved for the Soviet Union's greatest heroes. Red Square, where the Kremlin is located and where the cosmonaut would have been officially welcomed back from space if he had survived, was draped in mourning. Silent crowds watched the funeral procession as it crossed the square. At the Kremlin wall, government leaders made brief speeches of tribute to the dead spaceman. Speaking for his fellow cosmonauts, Yuri Gagarin pledged that they would continue the work for which Komarov had given his life.

Scenes from the funeral of Cosmonaut Vladimir Komarov in Moscow. Above, procession passes through Red Square. Below, bier and honor guard.

On March 27, 1968, Gagarin himself was killed in an airplane accident that also took the life of his copilot, Vladimir S. Seryogin. They were returning from a training flight when their jet crashed.

After his pioneering Vostok 1 mission, Yuri Gagarin had served as commander of the cosmonauts' group and deputy to the head of the Soviet space program commission. He was in charge of all Soviet projects involving lunar exploration.

One other Soviet cosmonaut had been killed in a training plane crash and another had died in a parachute accident.

In addition to the three astronauts who perished in the Apollo fire, the United States had lost four astronauts in aircraft accidents and one in an automobile crash.

The Soviet Union began an investigation of the Soyuz 1 mishap amid a flurry of conflicting stories about what had happened to the spaceship and its pilot. According to one account, Cosmonaut Komarov had been unable to leave orbit and was doomed to a slow death as he continued to circle the earth. Another version claimed that the cosmonaut had died of a heart attack early in the flight. One rumor had him burning to death during reentry. He was also reported to have landed in Czechoslovakia, in the United States, and in eastern Russia, where he had been seen wandering about the countryside. There were suggestions that the Soyuz 1 mission had been a troubled flight before the reentry process began with the craft tumbling out of control. According to this theory, the tumbling continued, or reappeared, after the firing of the retro-rockets, eventually causing the parachute lines to tangle.

Space experts agreed, however, that the official Soviet announcement was probably a correct account of what happened. While investigators probed into the reasons why it happened, there would be no more Soyuz flights. The Soyuz missions already planned for the summer were canceled. Like Project Apollo, the Soyuz program came to a halt.

Project Apollo was the first to resume manned space flights. Its Apollo 7 went into orbit on October 11, 1968. Two weeks later, on October 26, a manned Soyuz capsule left the launching pad at Tyuratam. It carried Cosmonaut Georgi T. Beregovoi into orbit.

At forty-seven, Cosmonaut Beregovoi was the oldest man to go into space. He was a veteran of thirty years' service with the Soviet Air Force, which he joined when he was seventeen. During World War II the future spaceman flew two hundred combat missions. His many wartime decorations and honors included the prestigious title Hero of the Soviet Union.

Cosmonaut Georgi T. Beregovoi.

Following the war, Beregovoi became one of Russia's leading test pilots. When he joined the cosmonaut detachment in 1964, he had participated in more than four thousand test flights. "Our detachment has no technically better trained pilot than Georgi," Cosmonaut Yuri Gagarin said of Beregovoi.

Radio Moscow's announcement that a manned Soyuz space-ship had once again gone into orbit created some confusion at first. The orbiting craft was called Soyuz 3. What had happened to Soyuz 2? Another announcement that evening solved the mystery when it described Soyuz 3's rendezvous with an unmanned

October 26, 1968, at the launch complex of Soyuz 3. Cosmonaut Beregovoi enters the elevator that will take him aloft to the cabin of the spacecraft.

craft that had left Tyuratam the previous day. The unmanned craft was Soyuz 2.

The pair of Soyuzes had been launched into nearly identical, almost circular orbits, ranging from 127 to 140 miles above the earth for Soyuz 3 and from 115 to 139 miles for Soyuz 2. Soyuz 3's inclination from the equator was 51.4 degrees. Soyuz 2's was 51.7 degrees.

During Soyuz 3's initial orbit it came within 650 feet of Soyuz 2. At that point Cosmonaut Beregovoi took over manual control of his ship to move even closer. No information was released on how close he came, however.

After the rendezvous, Beregovoi radioed: "The flight is passing according to the program. I am carrying out scientific experiments. The systems are functioning excellently. I feel well. I am in high spirits."

During his fifth circuit of the earth the cosmonaut moved forward to the ship's work compartment to continue his experi-

Soyuz 3 on the launch pad, as seen on TV.

ments. He also slept there during the several hours that Soyuz 3's orbital path took it too far from the Soviet Union for radio contact.

On his second day in orbit, the cosmonaut guided his spaceship to another rendezvous with Soyuz 2 that lasted for ninety minutes. He was testing Soyuz 3's manual control system, which consisted of a set of jet engines to speed it up or slow it down and another set to change its orbital path. Again, there was no announcement about how close he came to Soyuz 2, or if he had attempted to dock with the unmanned craft.

At the time of the Soyuz 3 flight, the United States had accomplished several manned dockings. The Soviet Union, on the other hand, had docked two unmanned satellites, but had yet to carry out that maneuver with a manned craft. However, observers doubted that Soyuz 3 would attempt to link up with Soyuz 2. Soyuz 3 carried only one cosmonaut. As a safety measure, a second cosmonaut should be on hand. In case the ships failed to separate after docking the second man might have to leave the spacecraft and manually separate them. After the tragic end of Soyuz 1, Soviet space officials probably wanted to test the craft with one cosmonaut before they tried a difficult two-man mission.

In addition to carrying out rendezvous maneuvers, Cosmonaut Beregovoi's activities included observations of the mysterious luminescent particles that other cosmonauts and the astronauts had seen in space. He also took pictures of the twilight horizons of the earth, clouds, and the earth's snow-covered areas. During his thirty-third orbit, the cosmonaut observed three forest fires and a very active line of thunderstorms over the equator.

Soyuz 3 carried four television cameras, two mounted inside the capsule and two outside. Soviet television stations showed both live and taped views of the Soyuz 3 interior and the panorama outside its windows. In one telecast, Beregovoi held up a small sign that read: "Hello, everybody." He was also seen leaning from his seat to look down at the earth. He gave a thumbs-up sign to express his pleasure at the view.

On October 28, following a radio command from the ground, Soyuz 2 left orbit and landed on the steppes of Kazakhstan. Meanwhile, everything continued to go well with Soyuz 3 and its passenger, who reported that he was eating with a good appetite, sleeping well, and carrying out his assigned tasks.

After sixty-four orbits of the earth and almost four full days in space, Cosmonaut Beregovoi began preparations for a return to earth. This was the maneuver that had ended in disaster for Soyuz 1 and Beregovoi must have thought about the fate of that craft and its pilot as he guided Soyuz 3 into position for retro-rocket firing. The rockets ignited and burned for 145 seconds, after which the cosmonaut's cabin separated from the rest of the ship and headed earthward. Soyuz 3's parachute operated perfectly, as did its final braking rocket. The spaceship came down to a gentle landing in the Kazakhstan recovery area to end a successful space flight.

Later, the cosmonaut reported that Soyuz 3 touched down very softly. Its parachutes began to drag it in a strong wind, but Beregovoi activated a special system to cut them off. "When I stepped down to the earth," he said, "I felt as though I was slightly intoxicated. I swayed as though in a gently rocking boat."

One of the cosmonaut's first acts after he left Soyuz 3 was to scoop up a handful of the snow that covered the landing site. "Good, though rather cold," he remarked to the villagers who had rushed to greet him. The official recovery party brought the cosmonaut a fur coat. He put it on and turned down the earflaps of

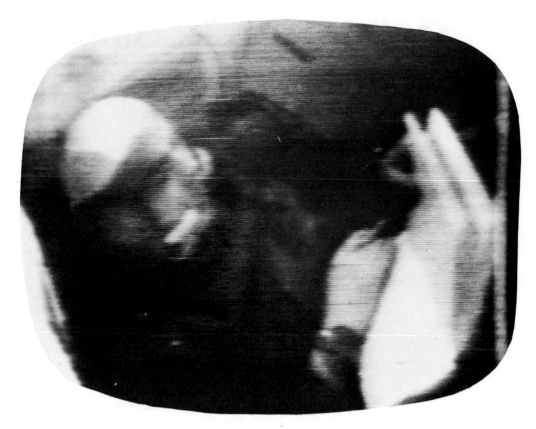

During his historic flight aboard Soyuz 3, Cosmonaut Beregovoi looked like this to Russian TV viewers.

his cap. The temperature was only 14 degrees Fahrenheit. After chatting with the villagers and signing autographs, the cosmonaut left in a helicopter.

Several days later during a press conference, Cosmonaut Beregovoi stated that Soyuz 3 could have held several men. "It would have been nice to have had a comrade," he remarked. "One pair of hands was hardly enough for all I had to do."

The cosmonaut revealed that both Soyuz 2 and Soyuz 3 were equipped for docking. He had not docked with Soyuz 2, however. "This was not on the program," he said.

Asked if he planned to make more flights into space the cosmonaut replied with a grin: "Of course!"

8 | SOYUZES IN ORBIT

In their speeches and writings during the 1960's, Soviet space officials often discussed the advantages of assembling space stations in orbit, an enterprise that would require multi-man crews and the docking of two or more spaceships. Although Soyuz 1 and Soyuz 3 carried only one cosmonaut each, the craft was big enough to carry more. And it was equipped for docking. Had the Soyuz been designed to transport cosmonauts and their equipment to a space station? Or was it intended for the long trip to the moon? In keeping with their policy of secrecy, the Russians revealed nothing definite about their plans for the Soyuz.

Meanwhile, the United States proceeded with its well-publicized space program. On December 21, 1968, two months after the Soyuz 3 mission, Apollo 8 set out on an epochal voyage around the moon.

While Apollo 8 traveled to the moon and back, preparations were under way at Tyuratam for a dual Soyuz launching. Soyuz 4, with Cosmonaut Vladimir Shatalov aboard, went into orbit on January 14. It was followed the next day by Soyuz 5. That craft carried three cosmonauts, Boris Volynov, Alexei Yeliseyev, and Yevgeny Khrunov.

Forty-one-year-old Vladimir Shatalov had been a backup pilot for the Soyuz 3 mission. The cosmonaut had grown up in Leningrad. He attended several Soviet Air Force schools and served as a pilot-instructor and as a jet pilot. He joined the cosmonaut detachment in 1963.

The fourteenth cosmonaut to orbit the earth wore a jacket and a fur cap to ward off the January cold when he arrived at the launching pad on the morning of Soyuz 4's departure from Tyuratam. During the prelaunch ceremonies, the cosmonaut said: "Two months have passed since my comrade and friend, Georgi Timofeyovich Beregovoi, made a four-day flight aboard the spaceship Soyuz 3. I have been intrusted with the task of continuing the tests of the excellent spaceship Soyuz."

Concluding his short speech with a cheery "Till I see you soon on dear earth," the cosmonaut boarded an elevator that carried him to the top of the tall booster where the Soyuz gleamed in the early morning light. With a final wave to his fellow cosmonauts and the officials who had gathered to see him off, Shatalov entered the spacecraft.

For the first time Russian television audiences saw a launching within ninety minutes of the actual blast-off. While American TV viewers were accustomed to seeing launchings at Cape Kennedy as soon as they happened, Soviet citizens waited days, or even weeks, before they saw films of their cosmonauts going into space. This time they saw the cosmonaut enter the elevator for the ride up to the Soyuz and wave when he reached the top platform. They also saw the last five minutes of the countdown, when service towers moved away from the rocket, the rocket's engines ignited, and the Soyuz 4 rose from its pad followed by a trail of fire.

Soyuz 4 entered an orbit that carried it from 107 to 140 miles above the earth's surface. This orbit was not a permanent one, however. During his fifth trip around the earth, Shatalov fired the Soyuz's maneuvering rockets to raise the ship's perigee to 129 miles and its apogee to 147 miles.

There were frequent television broadcasts from Soyuz 4. Shortly after the launching, a smiling Cosmonaut Shatalov told his audience: "I feel fine. Everything is working excellently." Shatalov was strapped to his couch in the Soyuz's command cabin, but he was not wearing a space suit. He assured his viewers that he had successfully withstood the strains of launching and adjusted well to weightlessness.

Two hours later the cosmonaut beamed another program to his fellow Russians. "I report to you with the help of inside and outside cameras," he said. "There are two outside cameras. Through television cameras I can observe other objects. Orientation can be carried out with the help of TV cameras.

"There is a TV camera in the orbital compartment also. It is a portable one. There is another camera inside the deck [command] cabin.

"Now in the second hour of my flight, I had my lunch according to the program. Further reporting will be done from the orbital compartment and I shall introduce you to the spacecraft's systems."

Soyuz 4 had completed sixteen orbits when Soyuz 5 left the launching pad at Tyuratam. The two ships quickly established radio contact. "I'll meet you soon in space," Cosmonaut Shatalov told the Soyuz 5 crew.

Soyuz's 5's commander, Boris Volynov, had joined the cosmonaut detachment at the same time as Yuri Gagarin. Prior to becoming a cosmonaut, Volynov was one of the Soviet Union's outstanding fighter pilots. Cosmonaut Volynov spent his boyhood in a Siberian mining town. After finishing secondary school there, he attended a flying school and an aviation college. While in the cosmonaut detachment, Volynov graduated from the Zhukovsky Air Force Engineering Academy. He served as a backup pilot for the Vostok 5 and the Soyuz 3 missions.

As a schoolboy in Moscow, Alexei Stanislavovich Yeliseyev, Soyuz 5's flight engineer, excelled in mathematics, physics, and the applied sciences. He completed his education at Moscow's Bauman Higher Technical College. Yeliseyev began working with problems of space technology in 1963. He was an engineer and designer. In 1966 he passed medical tests and joined the cosmonaut detachment.

The Soyuz 5's third crew member, Yevgeny Khrunov, grew up

Soyuz's 5 commander was Boris Volynov, shown here relaxing at a game of chess with a fellow cosmonaut.

Cosmonaut Yevgeny Khrunov was the third crew member of Soyuz 5.

on a farm. He studied agriculture in secondary school, but continued his education in air force training schools. Between 1956 and 1960, Khrunov served in the Soviet Air Force as a fighter pilot. He was considered an excellent flyer with a remarkable ability to handle machinery. Khrunov became a cosmonaut in 1960. In 1965, as Cosmonaut Alexei Leonov's backup man, he underwent extensive training for a walk in space.

The Soyuz 5 crewmen began appearing on Soviet TV shortly after they went into orbit. The cosmonauts showed viewers their roomy cabin, demonstrated some of the effects of weightlessness, and displayed samples of the packages and tubes that held their food.

Soyuz 5 was traveling in an orbit very similar to that of Soyuz 4, with its apogee 143 miles above the earth's surface and a perigee of 124 miles. The orbital plane of both ships was inclined 51 degrees 40 minutes from the equator. They traveled around the earth once every ninety minutes.

In the official announcement of the dual space mission, Soviet spokesmen said the two Soyuz craft would ''carry out a wide range of tests in the interaction of two orbiting spaceships.'' The announcement also stated that the Soyuz could be considered ''a basic model for future piloted ships capable of fulfilling various scientific and economic tasks in orbit of the earth.''

Were the Russians planning to dock Soyuz 4 and Soyuz 5? Space experts predicted that this time that important maneuver would be attempted. And they were right.

With their outstretched solar panels making them look like huge birds, the two spaceships slowly drew together. At first their maneuvers were controlled from the ground. When the distance between the craft had narrowed to 100 yards, Cosmonaut Shatalov took over the control of Soyuz 4. ''The alignment of the ships is proceeding,'' he reported as he cautiously guided Soyuz 4 toward Soyuz 5 at a speed of 12 feet a minute. ''I am heading straight for the socket,'' he announced.

During Soyuz 4's thirty-fourth orbit and the eighteenth for Soyuz 5, Shatalov nudged a probe on his craft's nose into a special docking collar on Soyuz 5. From Cosmonaut Volynov in Soyuz 5 came some words of caution. ''Easy, not so rough!'' he admonished. Volynov was joking, however; the docking was a smooth one.

''I've searched for you a long, long time and now I've found you,'' Shatalov radioed to Soyuz 5.

Firmly locked together in a linkup that included their electrical circuits and telephone lines, the two spaceships were traveling in an orbit that varied from 130 to 155 miles above the earth's surface. It was a feat that Tass, the news agency, hailed as "the world's first experimental cosmic station."

In Soyuz 4's command cabin, Cosmonaut Shatalov remained in his seat, monitoring the craft's systems. Meanwhile, Soyuz 5 bustled with activity. Aided by the ship's commander, Cosmonauts Alexei Yeliseyev and Yevgeny Khrunov donned white space suits and helmets. The suits were equipped with a leg pack containing breathing oxygen and heating and ventilating equipment. As the two men dressed, gloves and hose connections floated in the gravity-free cabin until they were needed.

Leaving Cosmonaut Volynov behind in the command cabin, the two space-suited cosmonauts crawled into Soyuz 5's orbital cabin. The hatch between the two sections was closed. In Soyuz 4 Cosmonaut Shatalov sealed himself in that ship's command cabin.

When Cosmonauts Khrunov and Yeliseyev had breathed enough pure oxygen to purge their bloodstreams of nitrogen (they had been breathing a mixture of nitrogen and oxygen in the command cabin), Khrunov opened Soyuz 5's hatch and floated out into space. A safety line still connected him to the Soyuz, however. Using a handrail, the cosmonaut worked his way over to Soyuz 4. That craft's hatch opened and he entered its orbital compartment as the docked ships passed high over South America.

Cosmonaut Yeliseyev had been watching his colleague from Soyuz 5's open hatch. Once Khrunov was safely inside the other craft, Yeliseyev left Soyuz 5 and followed Khrunov into Soyuz 4's orbital compartment. The two men took an hour to complete the transfer because they both paused in their move from one ship to the other to perform experiments and do some simple assembly work.

The space walkers waited in Soyuz 4's sealed orbital compartment until atmospheric pressure was restored. Then they removed their space suits and joined Cosmonaut Shatalov in the command compartment. The first men to transfer from one craft to another in space were also the first space mailmen. They delivered to Cosmonaut Shatalov letters Soyuz 5 had carried into orbit.

Four hours and thirty minutes after they had docked, Soyuz 4 and Soyuz 5 separated and slowly moved away from one another. They continued to orbit the earth, but followed slightly different paths. Soyuz 4's journey was almost over, however. On

This blurred but historic photo shows Cosmonaut Khrunov crossing over to the Soyuz 4 spacecraft.

January 17, Cosmonaut Shatalov's third day in space and the second for his two companions, the spacecraft left orbit after forty-eight circuits and reentered the earth's atmosphere.

Soyuz 4 landed in the Kazakhstan recovery area, now buried in deep January snows. It was the first time the Soviets had attempted a midwinter landing. Cosmonaut Beregovoi's Soyuz 3 flight had indicated that the spacecraft could make a precise descent from orbit and Soyuz 4 confirmed it. The ship landed where recovery crews were waiting in the 30-degree-below-zero cold with warm coats, boots, and fur-lined caps for the three spacemen.

Soyuz 5, with Cosmonaut Volynov now its sole occupant, continued to travel around the earth for one more day. After completing forty-nine orbits, it, too, headed earthward. The craft landed in Kazakhstan northwest of the site where Soyuz 4 had come down.

The four cosmonauts were reunited at Tyuratam, where they had their postflight medical checkups and debriefing. Cosmonaut Shatalov, for one, had enjoyed his three days in space. "I hope we will have more flights soon and at more frequent intervals," he said.

Like the other Soviet spacemen before them, the Soyuz 4 and 5 cosmonauts received a hero's welcome in Moscow. It began when they arrived at the city's Vnukovo Airport from Tyuratam. Guns boomed a salute, a band played the Soviet anthem, and children gave them flowers. The cosmonauts walked from their plane across the famous 100 yards of red carpet to be greeted by government leaders and to report on the success of their joint space mission.

Following the airport ceremony, the cosmonauts departed for Moscow's Kremlin Palace, where six thousand guests, including many scientists and space experts, waited to honor them. The cosmonauts traveled in a motorcade of twenty black limousines and the short trip proved an eventful one.

Riding in the lead car, an open vehicle, the cosmonauts were holding bouquets of flowers and waving at the crowds waiting near one of the entrances to the Kremlin. Suddenly shots rang out, apparently aimed at the second limousine in the motorcade in which Cosmonauts Georgi Beregovoi, Valentina Tereshkova, Andrian Nikolayev, and Alexei Leonov were riding. Later, police officials said that the gunman thought the second car contained government leaders. The cosmonauts were unharmed, but their driver was killed and an escorting motorcycle officer was injured. Police arrested the gunman, who was given a mental examination and found to be insane.

Because of the shooting, the Kremlin reception was delayed slightly. The Soyuz 4 and 5 cosmonauts appeared calm, however. Each gave a speech, as did Communist party leader Leonid I. Brezhnev, who hailed the success of the dual mission and stressed the international aspects of space exploration.

With the Soyuz 4 and 5 flight, the Soviet Union's space program took a big step forward. For the first time two manned spacecraft had docked and crewmen had transferred from one ship to another.

In the United States, preparations were under way for an even more significant accomplishment — Project Apollo's manned landing on the moon. In March, during the Apollo 9 mission, two astronauts tested the lunar module, a small spacecraft that had been developed to carry astronauts from the Apollo capsule to the moon's surface and back. In May, Apollo 10 repeated Apollo 8's flight around the moon. There was one big difference, however. Two of the three Apollo 10 astronauts piloted a lunar module to within 9.26 miles of the moon and then returned to their orbiting mother ship. And on July 20, Astronauts Neil Armstrong and Edwin Aldrin landed a lunar module on the moon, while Michael Collins waited in the command ship, Apollo 11. The astronauts spent twenty-one hours and thirty-eight minutes on the lunar surface.

The noted Russian scientist Leonid Sedov wrote of Project Apollo's acomplishment: "Mankind highly appreciates the achievement of the American specialists and the daring astronauts."

Even before the momentous moon landing, the Soviet Union had conceded that American astronauts would be the first to reach that satellite of the earth. As usual, the Russians said little about their own plans. However, they had indicated that they might concentrate on the building of space stations. It was a project they considered even more important than a landing on the moon.

The next Soviet space effort confirmed that country's interest in orbiting stations. It involved no less than three Soyuz spacecraft.

Soyuz 6 was the first of the "cosmic troika" to leave Tyuratam. It was launched at 2:10 P.M., Moscow time, on October 11, 1969, a rainy day at Tyuratam. Nine minutes after the blast-off, the craft entered an orbit that carried it a maximum distance of 139 miles above the earth. Its perigee was 115.6 miles.

According to the official announcement of the launching, an extensive series of scientific experiments had been planned for Soyuz 6. One experiment of "great importance," the announce-

A group photograph of Soviet cosmonauts who variously participated in the Soyuz 6, 7, and 8 missions. Seated (left to right) are: Valery Kubasov, Gregory Shonin, Vladimir Shatalov, and Alexei Yeliseyev. Standing (left to right) are: Viktor Gorbatko, Anatoly Filipchenko, and Vladislav Volkov.

ment said, involved the welding of materials in space in a condition of weightlessness.

Two cosmonauts went into space aboard Soyuz 6. The spacecraft commander was thirty-four-year-old Gregory S. Shonin, a former naval pilot, who thought of space flying as the logical continuation of aviation.

Shonin, a native of the Ukraine, had served as a pilot with the Soviet Baltic and Northern fleets before becoming a cosmonaut. He was an honors graduate of the Zhukovsky Air Force Engineering Academy and an admirer of the books of Antoine de Saint-Exupéry, the French pilot and author.

Soyuz 6's flight engineer, Valery N. Kubasov, had served as one of the backup cosmonauts for the Soyuz 5 mission. Before becoming a cosmonaut, he had earned a master's degree in technical sciences at the Moscow Aviation Institute and worked as a design engineer. The thirty-four-year-old Kubasov was an expert on spacecraft systems, ballistics, astronomy, and planetary physics.

Soyuz 6 traveled around the earth once every 88.36 minutes. Tass reported that both ship and crew were functioning normally. "According to medical telemetric information, the two cosmonauts feel well and have retained a great capacity for work. Medical experiments were carried out and geological and geographic objects of the earth were observed and photographed," the news agency said. The two men were also reported to have eaten a 6 P.M. dinner "with appetite."

Early the next afternoon a second spacecraft joined Soyuz 6 in orbit. Soyuz 7 was launched at 1:45, Moscow time, as Soyuz 6 was completing its sixteenth circuit of the earth. The two craft had the same orbital inclination, 51.7 degrees from the equator. The shape of their orbits varied slightly, however. Soyuz 6 was following an almost circular path that carried it from 141 to 143 miles above the earth's surface, while Soyuz 7 ranged from 121 to 134 miles above the earth.

Three cosmonauts went into space aboard Soyuz 7. The ship's commander, Anatoly Filipchenko, was a former pilot and test pilot who had flown approximately twenty different types of planes during his Soviet Air Force career.

Dark-haired Cosmonaut Filipchenko, called "Filip" by his friends, was a slender man of medium height. He was fond of sports, especially hunting and spear fishing.

Filipchenko joined the cosmonaut detachment in 1963. He served as a backup pilot for Soyuz 4. Of the Soyuz 7 mission he said: "Our dream is coming true."

Cosmonaut Vladislav Volkov, Soyuz 7's flight engineer, received his training at the Moscow Aviation Institute. He was working as an engineer when he learned that members of his profession were needed in the cosmonaut program. He applied and was accepted. When asked about his decision to become a cosmonaut, Volkov said: "I want to master space equipment, to test it and help in improving it, to do something resembling what test pilots now do in aircraft design offices." At the time of the Soyuz 7 flight, the cosmonaut was thirty-three years old.

Soyuz 7's third crew member was thirty-four-year-old Viktor Gorbatko, the mission's research engineer. He was a pilot in the Soviet Air Force before becoming a cosmonaut. In addition to completing the regular cosmonaut training program, Gorbatko was graduated from the Zhukovsky Air Force Engineering Academy. He was a backup pilot for the Soyuz 5 flight.

Soyuz 7's official mission included both technical and scientific activities. A Tass announcement said: "The crew has the task of maneuvering in orbit, staging joint navigational observations of the spaceships Soyuz 6 and Soyuz 7 in group flight, observation of celestial bodies and the horizon of the earth, determination of the real luminosity of the stars, observations of changes in illumination created by the sun, and other scientific experiments."

With five cosmonauts in orbit, one more than the United States had orbited during the Gemini 6 and 7 missions in 1965, many experts thought that the Soviet Union would try to construct some kind of a space laboratory, or at least test a procedure for building one. However, in a television broadcast from Soyuz 6, Cosmonaut Kubasov said his craft had no special equipment for docking. Moreover, it also lacked the automatic systems needed to move close to another craft. According to the cosmonaut, Soyuz 6 did carry large amounts of scientific equipment and extra fuel for maneuvering in space.

Soon after Soyuz 7 went into orbit, it was reported to be in group flight with Soyuz 6 and the two ships remained in adjacent orbits until they were joined by still another Soyuz on October 13.

Soyuz 8 carried two more cosmonauts into space, bringing the total number in orbit around the earth to seven. The latest additions to the group flight were both veteran spacemen. Vladimir A. Shatalov had piloted Soyuz 4 when it docked with Soyuz 5. Shortly after the Soyuz 8 launching, he was named commander of the seven-man space team.

Cosmonaut Shatalov's companion in Soyuz 8, Alexei S. Yeliseyev, had served as Soyuz 5's flight engineer. During that mission he had transferred to Soyuz 4 while the two ships orbited the earth.

In an interview before his second space journey, Cosmonaut Yeliseyev noted: "The emotional tension is less." And the Soyuz 8 mission did appear to be a trouble-free one. The craft was following the same general path as its sister ships. At its maximum altitude Soyuz 8 was 139 miles above the earth; its closest distance to the earth was 128 miles. It completed an orbit every 88.6 minutes.

During their second trip around the earth, Cosmonauts Shatalov and Yeliseyev ate beefsteak, bread, and chocolate and drank black currant juice. At approximately the same time the Soyuz 6 crew had a dinner of dried fish, pâté, chicken, bread, and prunes. In Soyuz 7, meat puree, veal, bread, and pastry were on the menu. After the spacemen had eaten, Commander Shatalov told the controllers on the ground: "The cosmonauts feel well."

Despite the fact that a record seven men and three spacecraft were now in orbit, the Soviet Union released little information about what the cosmonauts planned to do before they returned to earth. Brief announcements disclosed that the most recently launched Soyuz 8 crew had investigated the polarization of solar light as reflected by the earth's atmosphere. The three men in Soyuz 7 had made observations of the earth and photographed it and the stars, while in Soyuz 6 the cosmonauts had conducted medical and biological tests. Nothing was said about an attempt to link up at least two of the orbiting craft, but rumors persisted that an effort would be made to duplicate, and perhaps improve on, the successful docking of Soyuz 4 and 5.

On Soyuz 8's second day in space that craft and Soyuz 7 moved closer to each other to allow the crews to test the visibility of objects at varying distances in space. As the ships maneuvered, the cosmonauts made observations and took pictures. But the two ships did not dock. Instead, the cosmonauts continued with their observations and experiments. They conducted medical tests, photographed the earth, checked portholes and exterior optical systems for signs of erosion by micrometeorites, and tested maneuvering equipment. At one time Soyuz 7 and 8 were within 1,600 feet of one another, close enough for the cosmonauts to flash lights to test their visibility. Meanwhile, Soyuz 6 maneuvered nearby.

Soyuz 6's welding experiment took place on October 16. To prepare for it, Cosmonauts Shonin and Kubasov sealed themselves in the craft's command compartment and depressurized the adjoining orbital compartment. When a vacuum had been created, they activated an apparatus in the orbital compartment called Vulcan. While the cosmonauts watched through a window, Vulcan did the welding by remote control.

The spacemen tested three different welding techniques. One employed a high-energy arc, or current of electricity, between an electrode and the material being welded to melt and fuse the metal. The second used a low-pressure, ionized gas, or plasma, instead of the high-energy arc. A third method focused a beam of high-energy electrons on the metal to be welded, and this was the only method that produced a weld. The cosmonauts discovered that the other techniques would not work in the vacuum of space. The electronic beam, on the other hand, apparently could be used to assemble an orbiting station or to repair a spacecraft in flight.

Soon after the completion of the welding tests, when it had been in orbit for five days and completed eighty circuits of the earth, Soyuz 6's mission came to an end. The craft landed in the Soyuz recovery area near the city of Karaganda, where the first snow of the season had fallen.

Cosmonaut Shonin reported that he and his colleague felt fine. And they had enjoyed being part of the cosmic troika. "When you fly among the stars alone it is lonely," he said, "but when you are together with friends your spirits are high and you work well."

Soyuz 7 and Soyuz 8 continued to travel around the earth. They remained close to each other, but they did not dock. Space experts still expected them to do so, however. Otherwise, the cosmic troika mission would add little to the Soviet Union's knowledge of space-station-building techniques.

Any possibility that Soyuz 7 and 8 would dock vanished when Soyuz 7 returned to earth on October 17. During its five days in space the craft had completed eighty orbits. It landed in the same snow-covered area as had Soyuz 6.

Cosmonaut Filipchenko told newsmen who interviewed the returned space travelers that for him the most impressive sight from Soyuz 7 was the earth, especially "the sunrises and sunsets, which baffle description. One must see it for oneself," he said.

When newsmen observed that the cosmonauts seemed to walk with difficulty, Filipchenko said: "We got used to weightlessness quicker than we got used to the pull of gravity."

Soyuz 8, the only ship of the cosmic troika still in orbit, conducted an unusual communications experiment before it landed on October 18. When the craft was beyond direct radio contact with the Soviet Union, the cosmonauts kept in touch with the control center at Tyuratam with the help of a tracking ship in the Atlantic Ocean and an unmanned Soviet communications satellite, Molniya 1. The vessel was the *Vladimir Komarov*, named for the cosmonaut who was killed during the Soyuz 1 mission.

When it landed, Soyuz 8, like its sister ships, had orbited the earth eighty times in approximately 118 hours and 40 minutes. The three-ship mission, which spanned seven days, had carried out its program, Soviet spokesmen said. In addition to two space records — the most men and the most ships in space at the same time — they noted other achievements. The crews of the three ships had checked manually operated maneuvering facilities and tested systems of control in group flight. They had observed and photographed geological and geographical objects on the earth. And they had studied the effects of space flight on the human organism. Soyuz 6 had experimented with welding in space and Soyuz 8 had tried out a comunications relay system.

Nevertheless, the real purpose of the elaborate week-long mission remained in question. There was speculation that Soyuz 7 and 8 had tried to dock but could not do so because of mechanical or other problems. One Soviet official admitted: "Unanticipated situations arose that were new for both the cosmonauts and the ground control station. Solving these new problems gave us more information than merely repeating that which we already knew."

And Mission Commander Vladimir Shatalov added to the speculation when he said in a report: "There were, of course, difficulties, but we calmly dealt with them."

Officially, however, the multiple flight of Soyuz 6, 7, and 8 was hailed as a success and soon preparations were under way in Tyuratam's test and assembly building for the launching of Soyuz 9.

Like their counterparts at Cape Kennedy, Soviet technicians tested and assembled their spacecraft inside a huge building. Then they moved the assembled spacecraft and rocket to the launch site on a rail transporter whose locomotive carried the markings of the Russian state railway system. During the short journey, the spacecraft and rocket were horizontal. At the launching pad, giant cranes lifted the Soyuz and its booster to a vertical position.

Soyuz 9 was launched from a floodlit pad at an unusually late hour, 10:00 P.M., Moscow time, on June 1, 1970. It carried two cosmonauts, Flight Commander Andrian G. Nikolayev and Flight Engineer Vitaly I. Sevastyanov. In a statement before the launching, Cosmonaut Nikolayev said: "Today the crew of the spaceship Soyuz 9 leaves on a space trip to continue the important work of space exploration in the interests of national economy, science, and technology. Our country conducts in a planned way its work to conquer outer space. The crew of the spaceship Soyuz 9 is to carry out another stage of the program of scientific and technical research and experiments."

The Soyuz 9 spacecraft on its launch pad.

Nikolayev, who piloted Vostok 3 in 1962, was one of the best known of the cosmonauts. After the Vostok 3 mission he assisted with other Soviet space flights and helped develop the Soyuz spacecraft. He also earned a degree at the Zhukovsky Air Force Engineering Academy.

Vitaly Sevastyanov, Nikolayev's companion in Soyuz 9, studied aviation and space engineering at the Moscow Aviation Institute. While working toward an advanced degree, he gave a series of lectures on the theory of space travel to the cosmonauts. In 1965

Cosmonaut Vitaly Sevastyanov, flight engineer of Soyuz 9.

he began cosmonaut training himself and, with Cosmonaut Nikolayev, worked on plans for the Soyuz 9 flight.

As usual, the initial announcement of the Soyuz 9 launching
came only after the craft was safely in orbit. The statement was
brief: Soyuz 9 would carry out an extensive program of scientific
and technical research and experiments "in the conditions of a
solitary orbital flight." Soyuz 9 apparently was not going to be
joined by another craft while it circled the earth.

Soviet citizens were assured that the launching had gone normally and that the two cosmonauts were "feeling well." While in orbit they would be carrying out a busy work schedule that included biological, geological, and meteorological experiments and tests of the spaceship's navigation and control equipment.

During one of Soyuz 9's first control tests, Cosmonaut Nikolayev moved the craft into a new orbit. The maneuver was successful, but at its conclusion the spaceship's portholes were fogged. After analyzing the problem, Flight Engineer Sevastyanov concluded that it was caused by the firing of the ship's rocket engine.

At the time of the Soyuz 9 launching, American Astronaut Neil Armstrong, the first man to set foot on the moon, was visiting Star City, the Moscow suburb where the cosmonauts live. The astronaut had to watch the launching later on television, however. No Westerner had ever been present at a manned Soviet launching, although French President Charles de Gaulle had watched an unmanned research satellite leave Tyuratam.

After Soyuz 9 went into orbit Astronaut Armstrong sent a message to the cosmonauts wishing them a successful mission. He received a message of thanks in return.

Later Armstrong met with Premier Alexei N. Kosygin. The astronaut gave the premier a fragment of moon rock brought back by Apollo 11. It was a gift from the President of the United States. The premier also received a small Soviet flag that Apollo 11 had carried to the moon.

"Please convey to the American President my profound gratitude for this wonderful gift," the premier told the astronaut. "We will always cherish this gift as a symbol of great achievement. The Soviet government and Soviet people are second to none in admiring your great courage and knowledge."

Meanwhile, the two cosmonauts in the orbiting Soyuz 9 were observing and photographing the earth. They hoped to locate undiscovered mineral deposits and areas where melting snows might cause floods. The cosmonauts were also keeping a close check on their own physical condition and ability to work as their space journey lengthened. Soviet scientists were concerned about the effects of weightlessness and the spacecraft's artificial atmosphere on the two men. The success of a future space platform would depend on the ability of cosmonauts to live and work in orbit for long periods of time. At the end of Soyuz 9's twenty-second orbit Cosmonauts Nikolayev and Sevastyanov reported that they felt well and had lost none of their capacity to work.

As the hours passed and Soyuz 9 continued to circle the earth with no indication that the craft would soon land, speculation grew that it would be a long flight, longer than the Vostok 5 mission that had lasted 119 hours and 6 minutes in 1963 and perhaps longer than the record-breaking flight of the United States Gemini 7 that remained in space for 330 hours and 35 minutes in 1965.

Each day the cosmonauts spent two one-hour periods doing exercises designed to prevent degeneration of the muscles, bones, and the circulatory system that now had no gravity to work against. While they exercised, they monitored devices that checked their heart rates, blood pressures, respiration, and other vital functions. They also used a chest expander to test the sensitivity of their joints and muscles.

On one occasion ground controllers noted that the level of carbon dioxide in the spacecraft was low. Carbon dioxide is a by-product of human activity and the controllers guessed, correctly, that the cosmonauts had been cutting short their exercise periods. The spacemen explained that they had been too busy with experiments to complete all the exercises. "Do all your exercises, even at the expense of the experiments," the controllers ordered.

While exercising, Nikolayev and Sevastyanov wore an elastic harness that was connected at the waist to straps pulling them toward the floor. The tension, which simulated the weight of the human body on earth, made their muscles work harder.

To exercise their chest and shoulder muscles, the cosmonauts hauled at an elastic cord and their chest expander. The latter had a dial to show how hard they were pulling.

Previous cosmonauts had reported that colors did not seem as bright in space as they did on earth and the Soyuz 9 crew confirmed this. When they observed a variety of colored objects, they had difficulty recognizing some of the colors. In addition, their eye muscles coordinated poorly, possibly because of the effect of weightlessness on the muscles.

Although their workdays averaged sixteen hours, the cosmonauts found time to relax in the Soyuz's comfortable orbital compartment. In a news release describing the compartment, Tass said: "A convenient sofa stands in one end of the cabin. Opposite is a working office with a table and sideboard. Finished in mahogany, they are handsome and harmonious."

From the orbital compartment, Nikolayev and Sevastyanov played a long-distance chess match with the Soyuz ground crew. It ended in a draw on the thirty-sixth move.

On June 6, Soyuz 9 broke the Soviet record for time in space set by Cosmonaut Bykovsky when he orbited the earth for five days in Vostok 5. However, Soyuz 9 would have to remain aloft for another eight days and nineteen hours in order to better Gemini 7's record for prolonged space flight. No date had been set for the end of the Soyuz 9 mission, but the craft was equipped to support its two-man crew for eighteen days.

On Soyuz 9's twelfth day in space Cosmonaut Nikolayev reported that he and his flight engineer were somewhat tired. They were still carrying out their busy work program, although they had to shorten their afternoon rest periods — two hours after lunch — to get everything done.

The cosmonauts' day began when it was 1 P.M. at the Tyuratam cosmodrome and ended between four and five o'clock the next morning. This schedule had been worked out to accommodate Soyuz 9's late-night launch, which, in turn, was selected to allow the craft to land in daylight at the end of its mission. During pre-flight training, the cosmonauts had practiced the work-rest pattern that they followed in space.

At 10 P.M., Moscow time, on June 15, Soyuz 9 had been in orbit exactly fourteen days, a new record for continuous manned space flight. The cosmonauts were reported to be in good health and there was no indication that their mission was near its end. From NASA's Manned Spacecraft Center in Houston, Texas, where they had been following the Soyuz 9 flight with considerable interest, Frank Borman and James A. Lovell, the astronauts who had held the space endurance record for almost five years, sent a message to Cosmonauts Andrian Nikolayev and Vitaly Sevastyanov. "We congratulate you and pass on our best wishes as you pass new milestones in space exploration," the Americans said.

While Soviet officials noted the number of hours their latest manned spacecraft had remained aloft, they gave little publicity to the new record. Instead, they emphasized that Soyuz 9, like the earlier Soyuz missions, was preparing the way for the launching of a space station, where cosmonauts would carry out experiments over long periods of time and from which they would set out on journeys to outer space.

Soyuz 9 remained in orbit for 17 days 16 hours 59 minutes. In that time it traveled more than 7,000,000 miles and made 287 circuits of the earth. The craft was in orbit about 6,000 miles away from its recovery area when the landing process began. In spite of the great distance it had to travel, Soyuz 9 touched down right on target, 47 miles west of the city of Karaganda in Kazakhstan.

Recovery teams with planes, helicopters, and parachutists

The two cosmonauts aboard Soyuz 9 in flight, as monitored on TV.

were waiting for Soyuz 9. The first search-plane pilot to see the descending space capsule radioed: "I have spotted the target and am closing in on it."

The cosmonauts had evidently been on the lookout for the recovery aircraft. They radioed: "We see the plane on the right."

One of the helicopter pilots sent in the next report. "I have spotted the vehicle. It is moving in the set direction. The helicopter group is preparing to land."

Another helicopter pilot sent the message the control center at Tyuratam was waiting for. "The cosmonauts have landed safely," he reported. "They have stepped down from the ship and were taken aboard one of the helicopters."

Initial reports on the health of the cosmonauts after their long space journey were favorable, although recovery crews noted that both men looked pale and haggard. A bulletin issued by Tass shortly after the landing said: "A quick medical checkup of the cosmonauts showed that they had withstood the prolonged space flight well."

During the ensuing ten days, the spacemen were given more extensive physical examinations in a special, germ-free apartment on the outskirts of Moscow, where they were isolated from possible sources of infection. From the examinations, Russian scientists learned that the problem of adaptation to an extended period of weightlessness was a complex one.

Immediately after their return to earth after almost eighteen days in space, the cosmonauts were unable to walk without help. Moreover, they found it hard to stand upright. Sleeping was difficult also. When lying down, they felt as if a great weight was pushing through them to their backs. "We did not anticipate that it would be so difficult to adjust our limbs and other parts of the body," Cosmonaut Nikolayev conceded.

Comparing the Soyuz 9 mission to his ninety-four-hour flight in Vostok 3, the cosmonaut said: "The return to earth from Soyuz 9 after such a long time in space is more difficult."

After three days back on earth Cosmonaut Nikolayev still weighed 2.2 pounds less than he had before the flight. Cosmonaut Sevastyanov was 4.4 pounds lighter. The cosmonauts' cardiovascular systems were within normal limits, although doctors had observed what they termed "a certain instability" in both men.

Eleven days after the flight the cosmonauts were able to return to near-normal physical activity. However, Soviet spokesmen remained cautious in their statements about man's ability to survive long periods of weightlessness. Soyuz 7 commander, Anatoly Filipchenko, told a reporter: "To a certain extent, the forecast of scientists was confirmed, that man in a long flight will get used to weightlessness and will be able to work fruitfully. For future experiments that may last more than one month, it must be known precisely to what limit weightlessness is permissible."

A Soviet physician said that he thought the exercise program followed by Cosmonauts Nikolayev and Sevastyanov during their almost eighteen days in space helped their muscles to some extent. "But the measures were not sufficient," he added.

Soviet scientists had expected some of the difficulties the cosmonauts experienced after the Soyuz 9 flight and they did not think them serious enough to rule out longer space missions. Rather, they considered Soyuz 9 to be a successful step toward what was now Russia's goal for manned space flight: the construction of orbital stations.

9 | UNMANNED EXPLORERS

While the cosmonauts orbited the earth in Vostok, Voskhod, and Soyuz spaceships, the Soviet Union was also launching a large number of unmanned satellites and space probes. In the ten years following the launching of the first Sputnik, more than two hundred unmanned satellites went into orbit and others followed in succeeding years. The satellites served a variety of purposes. Some were communications satellites that transmitted Soviet radio and TV programs. Many were research vehicles that gathered information about the upper atmosphere and the effects of space on various forms of life. Still others photographed the earth for scientific or military purposes. Meanwhile space probes were going to the moon and to Venus and Mars.

Perhaps the most successful of the Soviet Union's unmanned programs was the one designed to gather information about the moon. After Luna 1 went past the moon, Luna 2 crash-landed on its surface, and Luna 3 went into lunar orbit, the program continued with Luna 4. Launched in April, 1963, it missed the moon by some 5,000 miles. Although the Soviet Union made no definite statement about Luna 4's mission, it may have been an attempt at a soft landing on the lunar surface. In a soft landing a space vehicle comes down so gently that its delicate instruments continue to relay information to the earth after the landing. A hard, or crash, landing, while easier to accomplish, destroys the spaceship and its instruments.

Instead of landing on the moon, the 3,135-pound Luna 4 went into a deep earth orbit and eventually into an orbit around the sun.

When Luna 5 was launched in May, 1965, the Soviets announced that the craft would attempt a soft landing on the moon. Luna 5 reached the moon after three and a half days of flight. Its braking rockets failed, however, and it crashed in the moon's Sea of Clouds.

A month later Luna 6, probably a repeat of the Luna 5 mission, had engine trouble en route to the moon. It sped off into a solar orbit, missing the moon by more than 99,000 miles.

Luna 9 was launched on January 31, 1966. It made the first soft landing on the moon and relayed TV pictures of the lunar surface back to earth.

Luna 7 left its launching pad at Tyuratam on the eighth anniversary of the first Sputnik. However, Luna 7 was not as successful as the Sputnik. When it reached the vicinity of the moon, its braking rockets fired too soon and the craft made a hard, rather than a soft, landing. Although it sent no data from the lunar surface, it did relay information during its journey to the moon.

Unfortunately, Luna 8, launched in December, 1965, repeated the Luna 7 mission, including the hard landing.

Soviet spacemen may have been discouraged by the many difficulties they encountered in their attempts to land Lunas on the moon, but they continued to try. With Luna 9, launched on January 31, 1966, their efforts were rewarded. The craft, which was aimed at the moon's western edge, approached the lunar surface on February 3. When it was 47 miles above the moon, ground controllers fired braking rockets for forty-eight seconds. The timing of the maneuver was of the greatest importance. If the craft was slowed too soon or too late, it would crash. Likewise, the braking rocket had to fire for the precise time required to slow Luna 9 to the near-zero speed that would insure a soft landing.

Four minutes and ten seconds after it touched down in the moon's Ocean of Storms, Luna 9 began to send radio signals, and Russian scientists knew that they had achieved a successful soft landing.

What landed on the moon was a sphere about 2 feet in diameter. A midcourse guidance and propulsion section had been jettisoned on the way to the moon. The craft separated from its descent control system just before landing.

The first instrument package to survive a landing on the moon resembled a large flower. It had four petal-like sections that folded down to expose the upper half of the sphere. Four antennas extended from the open section to relay information back to the earth.

During the three days that its power supply lasted, Luna 9 took television pictures of the lunar surface and collected data on radiation. More than three years before the first man reached the moon, Luna 9's pictures indicated that the moon, at least in the Ocean of Storms area, was not covered with a thick layer of dust into which a cosmonaut or astronaut would sink. Instead, it appeared to have a porous, pitted surface dotted with craters and small rocks.

The next Luna left for the moon two months later. The early part of its flight duplicated that of Luna 9, but Luna 10's midcourse correction aimed it at a precise point behind the moon. When the speeding capsule reached its destination, ground controllers, 240,000 miles away, slowed it to a speed of 2 miles a second. At that velocity, Luna 10 was captured by the moon's gravity and it became the first artificial satellite of the earth's satellite, a remarkable achievement.

Circling the moon in an orbit that ranged from 217 to 261

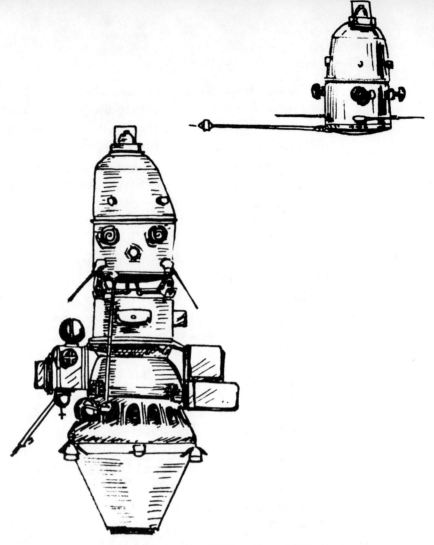

Sketches of Luna 10 (left) and its payload (right) after separation.

miles above the lunar surface, Luna 10 measured the moon's magnetic field and took readings that indicated the moon's surface was basaltic, like the earth. The craft's instruments also revealed that it was being bombarded with micrometeorites.

For four hundred and sixty orbits over fifty-seven days Luna 10 transmitted its instrument readings to the earth. When its power supply was exhausted, it fell silent, although it continued to travel around the moon.

Luna 10 sent no pictures back to earth and neither did Luna 11, launched in August, 1966, to repeat Luna 10's mission. Luna 12, in October, 1966, carried a television camera into an orbit around the moon that came to within 62 miles of the surface at its closest point. Russia's second moon satellite photographed the lunar terrain, while its instruments measured radiation and micrometeoroid activity.

With Luna 13, launched in December, 1966, Soviet spacemen resumed their study of the moon from its surface. The craft resembled Luna 9, but engineers had added two 5-foot booms that deployed from the midsection after a successful soft landing in the Ocean of Storms. One of the booms carried a soil density meter at its tip; the other had a device to measure radiation. Luna 13 was equipped with other measuring devices and a television camera system.

From Luna 13 Russian scientists learned that lunar soil resembled that of the earth, although it seemed to be less dense. They also discovered that the moon apparently absorbed most of the cosmic rays that fell on it.

The Soviet Union's Luna spacecraft were the first to travel to the moon, but unmanned lunar explorers launched by the United States soon joined them. The first of the United States programs, called Ranger, began in 1961. Ranger spacecraft were equipped with six television cameras with which they photographed the moon before making a hard landing.

After five failures, Ranger 6, launched in January, 1964, landed

The Luna 13 space probe's nomenclature: (1) petal antennae; (2) bayonnet antennae; (3) instrument brackets; (4) mechanical ground meter; (5) radiational density meter; and (6) television camera.

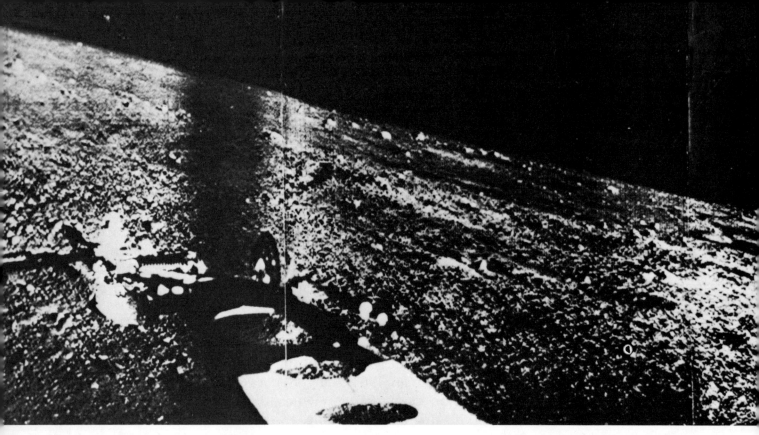

A panorama of the lunar surface as transmitted back to earth by the Luna 13 space probe.

on the moon. However, it failed to send back any pictures. The next three Rangers more than made up for the early failures. They sent back many excellent pictures of the lunar surface.

From the hard-landing Ranger craft the United States progressed to a more advanced program called Surveyor. Surveyors were designed to make soft landings on the moon, and the very first Surveyor was successful in June, 1966, some four months after Luna 9's soft landing. Five Surveyor craft out of seven made soft landings after which they photographed the moon's surface and tested its soil.

At the same time that Surveyors were landing on the moon, other United States craft traveled around that body. Called Lunar Orbiters, they were flying photographic laboratories that searched for the best places for manned landings on the moon. The first Lunar Orbiter was launched in August, 1966, when Luna 10 had been traveling around the moon for four months. During the next year, four more Lunar Orbiters circled the moon. When the project ended they had photographed 99 percent of the moon's surface.

With the successful conclusion of its Lunar Orbiter series, the United States concentrated on preparations for a manned landing on the moon, while the Soviet Union continued its unmanned ex-

ploration of the earth's satellite. Luna 14, launched from Tyuratam in April, 1968, was another lunar orbiting mission, as was Luna 15, launched on July 13, 1969. The latter had a more difficult flight plan, however. It was equipped with a navigation and maneuvering system that made possible a change of orbit as it traveled around the moon. Moreover, the craft was much larger than earlier Lunas; its weight was estimated at more than 6,000 pounds.

Luna 15 began to orbit the moon on July 17. Two days later its orbit changed on command from the earth and on the following day it was changed again. When the craft had completed fifty-two orbits, ground controllers fired retro-rockets to bring the craft down to the lunar surface. Although a soft landing was probably planned for Luna 15, it crash-landed instead.

Three days after Luna 15 left the launching pad at Tyuratam, Apollo 11, with its crew of three astronauts, set out for the moon from Cape Kennedy. Luna 15 was already traveling around the moon when Apollo 11 began a moon orbit of its own prior to the separation of the lunar-landing craft, *Eagle*, from the Apollo capsule, *Columbia*. While Astronauts Neil Armstrong and Edwin Aldrin were on the moon's surface, Luna 15 continued to orbit, but they could not see it. Neither could Astronaut Michael Collins who remained in lunar orbit in *Columbia*. Two hours before the Amer-

The Luna 16 space probe as photographed during experiments on earth.

ican spacemen left the moon's surface, Luna 15 crashed about 500 miles from the Apollo landing site.

Luna 16, launched on September 12, 1970, was further proof that the Soviet Union planned to continue unmanned exploration of the moon. The one-ton craft went into lunar orbit and then, following computer instructions received from the earth, descended to the lunar surface. It landed in the Sea of Fertility, 200 miles from Apollo 11's landing site.

After Luna 16's successful touchdown, a mechanical "hand" holding a power drill extended from the craft toward the lunar surface. Its movements were directed by controllers on the ground who probably had the Luna's television pictures to help them. The drill burrowed 14 inches into the moon to obtain a sample of its rocks and soil, which the hand placed in a container that was then sealed and stored in the upper half of the mooncraft.

Following a timetable carefully calculated to bring Luna 16's upper portion back to its designated landing area on earth, ground controllers ignited the craft's upper-stage rocket. Leaving its lower stage on the moon to transmit information about lunar temperatures and radiation, Luna 16 started on its long homeward journey. The successful return to earth ended in Kazakhstan when the canister containing the samples of lunar soil was recovered by helicopter search crews. Luna 16's mission, from launch to recovery, lasted twelve days.

The world's scientists were interested to learn that the 3½ ounces of lunar material collected by Luna 16 had a chemical content similar to the samples collected in the Ocean of Storms by the astronauts of the United States Apollo 12 moon mission. This was true in spite of the fact that the two landing sites were 1,000 miles apart. Apollo 11's landing site was located roughly between the other two, but its samples proved to have a different chemical composition. Scientists speculated that most of the moon's surface might resemble the Luna 16 and Apollo 12 samples.

Luna 16 provided scientists with another subject to discuss: Could unmanned space exploration provide almost as much information as the much more expensive manned space missions? Some United States space experts argued that the astronauts' personal observations and on-the-spot decisions were invaluable. Russian scientists, on the other hand, tended to favor unmanned probes, which endangered no lives and were twenty to fifty times cheaper. Moreover, distant planets would be beyond the reach of human explorers for many years to come.

Discussing the possibility of exploring the planets, Russian scientist Petrov said: "Automatic craft, capable of carrying out active experiments at a great distance and perhaps returning to earth, are indispensable for this."

On November 17, 1970, Luna 17 landed in the moon's Sea of Rains. It was a heavier craft than Luna 16 and its design was different as well. Above its engines and tanks Luna 17 carried what looked like a bathtub on wheels. After the landing, a ramp automatically extended from the Luna and the strange-looking contraption, acting on a command from the earth, rolled down to the

The launch vehicle used to boost Luna 17 into orbit as seen during installation operations.

moon's surface. Constructed largely of magnesium alloy, it was about the size of a small automobile with four spoked wheels on each side.

Later that day the Soviet Union announced that it had successfully landed a self-propelled vehicle on the moon. Its name was Lunokhod, the Russian equivalent of Moon Rover.

Tass described the beginning of the Lunokhod's moon mission. "Its first motions on the moon were not timid," Tass reported. "The vehicle immediately started on a series of scientific and technological investigations, and with the help of television cameras aboard the vehicle, the landing stage of the craft and the lunar surface on the landing site were viewed. The vehicle set out on an expedition in the Sea of Rains."

Each of the Lunokhod's eight wheels had its own motor. Power came from batteries charged by the sun's rays. If one of the wheels became stuck in a rut, it would automatically lose power while the other wheels pulled it free. Another automatic system stopped the vehicle if it started on a path too steep to be negotiated safely.

Most of the time, however, an earthbound crew that consisted of a commander, driver, engineer, navigator, and radio operator controlled the Lunokhod's movements. They did this with the help of television pictures transmitted by the craft as it moved along. The pictures covered a limited area and the controllers had to allow for the time it took signals to travel from the moon to the earth and back again. Nevertheless, the "driver" was able to keep the Lunokhod bumping over the lunar surface, 248,547 miles away. All of the team members had trained extensively for the Luna 17 mission using a model of the Lunokhod, which they directed over 60 miles of moon-like terrain.

In addition to its television cameras, Lunokhod 1 carried radios, an X-ray telescope, an X-ray spectrometer to analyze the lunar soil, and an array of mirrors built by French scientists to catch and reflect laser light signals beamed from the earth. By carefully checking the time it takes laser beams to travel, scientists can accurately measure distances.

Luna 17 touched down on the western shore of the Sea of Rains, the largest circular sea on the moon. From the landing site, Lunokhod 1 moved to the southeast across a fairly level area. Tass reported: "The self-propelled vehicle encountered rocks and comparatively small craters and overcame a lunar ridge that was not very high." As it traveled the Lunokhod measured the ease of its own movement.

After four earth days of operation on the moon, Lunokhod 1 maneuvered into a parking place to prepare for the lunar night. The moon's "days" and "nights" are two weeks long. During the two weeks of darkness there would be no sun to charge the craft's batteries. Moreover, temperatures would drop so low that the Lunokhod had to be protected by an atomic heater and special insulation.

Lunokhod 1 successfully survived the lunar night and went back into action with the return of sunlight to the Sea of Rains. "Early morning" on the moon lasts about two earth days. During that time the Lunokhod's controllers opened the craft's lid to allow its batteries to be recharged by the sun's rays. After checking the vehicle's systems to make sure that none had been damaged by the extreme cold, the controllers moved the Lunokhod from its parking place for more exploring. At high noon on the moon, when the absence of shadows made it difficult to distinguish objects on the lunar surface, its earthbound driver parked the Lunokhod. The craft resumed its travels when shadows reappeared to mark the

beginning of the lunar "afternoon." The Lunokhod's second lunar day ended as darkness returned to the Sea of Rains.

During its third lunar workday, Lunokhod 1 returned to the Luna 17 landing site. Because they knew the exact location of the site, the ground controllers were able to test the precision and reliability of the Lunokhod's navigation system. The controllers did not send the Lunokhod back over the same route, however. Instead, they selected a path that enabled their craft to explore a new stretch of the moon's terrain.

When its third lunar workday ended, the Lunokhod had traveled a total distance of 4,000 yards. Soviet scientists announced that they were pleased with the performance of the mooncar, which they hoped would function for many more lunar workdays.

Lunokhod 1 continued to operate until October, 1971, when its atomic heater wore out in the middle of a lunar night. During its active life, the robot mooncar traveled 6.5 miles, mapped 95,000 square yards of the lunar surface, tested the moon's soil, and took thousands of photographs.

In February, 1972, Luna 20 returned more lunar material to the Soviet Union. Its sample of the moon's soil, collected about 75 miles from Luna 16's landing site, resembled ash-colored dust with a few larger particles embedded in it.

While the Lunas were going to the moon, a second Soviet spacecraft, called Zond, carried out some moon missions. Zond 3, launched in July, 1965, sent pictures back to earth as it flew past the moon. Zond 5, equipped with cameras and biological experiments, traveled around the moon in September, 1968. It returned to earth and landed in the Indian Ocean in one of the Soviet Union's few water recoveries. Zond 5 and later Zonds were similar in design to the Soyuz spacecraft, although the Zonds carried cameras instead of cosmonauts.

The Soviet Union's planetary exploration program began in 1961 with an unsuccessful attempt to reach Venus. Venera 1, the first spacecraft to be aimed at that planet, came within 60,000 miles of its goal. Venera 2, launched in 1965, also missed Venus, but by only 15,000 miles. Venera 3, another 1965 mission, reached the distant planet after a 106-day, 24,000,000-mile journey. It failed to eject instruments designed to measure atmospheric pressure

Two drawings of Lunokhod 1, the Soviet lunar self-propelled vehicle, as landed successfully on the moon by Luna 17. Top photo depicts Lunokhod just landed; lower photo, the vehicle disembarks from the mother ship.

The Venera 4 spacecraft in its shed prior to launch. It made the first controlled descent on the planet Venus's surface.

and surface temperature, but it represented an amazing feat of navigation.

Venera 4, weighing a hefty 2,433 pounds, set out for Venus in June, 1967. It carried an insulated instrument package that left the main spacecraft and traveled separately through the hostile Venusian atmosphere. Until radio signals were lost after ninety-six minutes, Venera 4's instruments supplied information about Venus.

Scientists learned that the planet's surface temperature was over 500 degrees Fahrenheit and that its atmosphere was fifteen to twenty-two times as heavy as the earth's. The Venusian atmosphere contained large amounts of carbon dioxide, but little nitrogen, and the planet had only a weak magnetic field.

Venera 5 and Venera 6 reached Venus on May 16 and 17, 1970.

The Venera 7 spacecraft shown here during its development stage.

They were reported to have made a "smooth descent." Information radioed back as the two Veneras approached the planet's surface indicated that temperatures on Venus might reach 1,400 degrees Fahrenheit, while its atmospheric pressure was up to one hundred and forty times that of the earth. It is no wonder that Soviet scientists concluded: "This planet is not fit for human life."

American Venus probes had flown past the planet without trying to land and none of the Soviet Union's Veneras had succeeded in making a soft landing. Late in 1970, however, Venera 7's landing apparatus descended safely through the planet's atmosphere and for twenty-three minutes the instrument capsule sent out radio signals. It was the first time that information from the surface of another planet had ever been received on the earth. Venera 7's information differed somewhat from that sent by earlier Veneras. Its instruments indicated that the temperature on the surface of Venus was near 877 degrees Fahrenheit. The Venusian atmospheric pressure was ninety times that of earth.

Venera 7 was a significant achievement for Soviet scientists, who were also trying to send a spacecraft to the planet Mars. Mars 1, launched in 1962, traveled 66,000,000 miles toward Mars before radio contact was lost. Zond 2, launched in 1964, suffered a similar fate en route to Mars. In July, 1965, the United States Mariner 4 sent back the first close-up photographs of the planet. On November 14, 1971, the United States Mariner 9 became the first man-made satellite of another planet when it went into a looping orbit around Mars. The Soviet craft Mars 2, launched on May 19, 1971, reached Mars on November 27, 1971, and began to orbit that planet after ejecting a capsule containing an emblem displaying the Soviet hammer and sickle. The capsule probably crash-landed on the Martian surface. The Soviet Union's Mars 3 accomplished the first soft landing on Mars when it released a scientific space robot before going into Mars orbit on December 2, 1971. The robot sent signals for only twenty seconds after landing, however.

Not all of the Soviet Union's unmanned spacecraft travel to the moon or the planets. Many of them carry out their missions in earth orbit. For several years Molniya communications satellites have been relaying television and radio programs, telephone and telegraph messages, and newspaper-page facsimiles over the vast distances of the Soviet Union.

Meteor satellites, equipped with television cameras to photograph the earth's daytime cloud cover and infrared scanners to make nighttime measurements, provide the Soviet Union with meteorological and radiation data.

The Soviet Union has launched hundreds of earth satellites with the name Cosmos. The craft has had several configurations and many different kinds of missions. Cosmos craft have made weather observations. They have carried instruments to study the upper atmosphere and the earth's radiation belts. Some of them have carried animals into space and others have had secret military missions.

Several Cosmos satellites preceded the ill-fated Soyuz 1 into orbit to test the new spacecraft and its equipment. And they prepared the way for the cosmonauts who orbited the earth in later Soyuz missions.

10 | AN ORBITING LABORATORY FOR THE COSMONAUTS

No one was surprised when Mstislav V. Keldysh, the president of the Soviet Academy of Sciences, announced that the Soviet Union's manned space program would concentrate exclusively on building and launching space platforms. To newsmen who asked him if the Soviet Union had given up its plans to send cosmonauts to the moon, Keldysh said: "We have nothing to give up because we have never announced such a program. As we have said several times before, we are not going to fly to the moon in the nearest future."

When Keldysh made his announcement in July, 1970, the United States had already placed four astronauts on the lunar surface, and the Russians could only hope to be the second nation to accomplish a moon landing.

Several months passed before the Soviet Union launched its first space platform. It was a 17½-ton unmanned scientific laboratory to which the Russians gave the name Salyut (the word means "salute"). Salyut left Tyuratam on April 19, 1971, and went into an orbit ranging from 124 to 138 miles above the earth. Their orbiting laboratory was a new type of spacecraft, the Russians announced. Using its facilities, cosmonauts would be able to carry out a large number of valuable scientific and technological studies. "The on-board systems, equipment, and scientific apparatus of the station are functioning normally," the Russians said after the launching.

While the Salyut traveled around the earth, technicians at Tyuratam were preparing a Soyuz craft to join it in space. They launched Soyuz 10 before dawn on April 23. The fact that the three-man Soyuz crew included two veteran space travelers indicated that the mission would be an important one.

Soyuz 10's commander, Cosmonaut Vladimir Shatalov, had been at the controls of Soyuz 4 when it docked with Soyuz 5 in January, 1969. Later that year he commanded Soyuz 8 in its group flight with Soyuz 6 and Soyuz 7.

Cosmonaut Alexei Yeliseyev, the flight engineer of Soyuz 10, had previously been Soyuz 5's flight engineer. During that mission

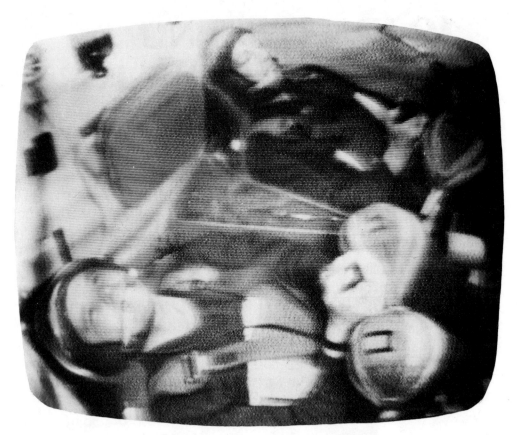

Cosmonauts Shatalov and Rukavishnikov are shown here during flight aboard Soyuz 10.

he "walked" over to Soyuz 4 to join Cosmonaut Shatalov for the trip back to earth. He traveled with Shatalov a second time during the Soyuz 8 mission.

Thirty-eight-year-old Cosmonaut Nikolai Rukavishnikov was making his first space trip in Soyuz 10. A graduate of the Moscow Engineering Physics Institute, where he studied automation and instrument making, Rukavishnikov began cosmonaut training in 1967. He was Soyuz 10's test engineer and his fellow cosmonauts predicted that his tinkering abilities might be needed during the flight.

Soyuz 10 went into an orbit that ranged from 130 to 154 miles above the earth. This was higher than the Salyut's orbit and Flight Commander Shatalov radioed the controllers at Tyuratam: "Looks like you threw us up a bit too high. Well, it doesn't matter. We'll fix it."

A brief firing of Soyuz 10's engines successfully lowered the craft's orbit. Instructions for the firing were relayed to the cosmo-

A portrait of Cosmonaut Nikolai Rukavishnikov.

nauts by a tracking ship in the Atlantic Ocean because the Soyuz had moved beyond the radio range of tracking stations in the Soviet Union.

Two hours after adjusting their orbit the cosmonauts began a rest period. While they slept, Russian television audiences saw a filmed prelaunch press conference during which Commander Shatalov said Soyuz 10 would continue the "important cause of exploring outer space in the interests of science and the nation's economy." Flight Engineer Alexei Yeliseyev told the reporters: "We have now started a new stage in space exploration connected with the preparation of orbital stations."

A drawing of the Soyuz spacecraft docking with the orbital scientific station Salyut.

TV viewers also saw Soyuz 10's predawn launching and shots of the cosmonauts at work in their spacecraft.

After a forty-one-hour chase, Soyuz 10 caught up with the orbiting Salyut. Automatic controls brought the Soyuz to within 590 feet of the space laboratory. Then Cosmonaut Shatalov took over and manually guided the craft the rest of the way. "The orbital space station Salyut looked overwhelming," Alexei Yeliseyev said later. "I don't even know what to compare it with. It was . . . a little like a train entering a railroad terminal. That's how we felt as our rather big Soyuz eased up to the station."

What the cosmonauts saw as they approached the Salyut was a gleaming, 60-foot-long cylindrical craft, which may have been converted from one of the stages of a Soviet rocket. Two pairs of solar panels extended from the craft. The Salyut's docking mechanism was located in its nose, and Cosmonaut Shatalov steered the Soyuz toward it.

Soyuz 10 accomplished its linkup with the Salyut while the two ships were beyond the radio range of Soviet tracking stations. However, the cosmonauts were able to communicate with ground controllers with the help of tracking vessels in the Atlantic and a Molniya satellite. They reported that Soyuz 10's systems were working normally after the docking. The controllers received similar information from the Salyut's instruments.

Space observers waited for word that one, or perhaps two, of the cosmonauts had moved from the Soyuz to the orbiting laboratory, but no crew transfer took place. Instead, after five and a half hours of docked flight, Soyuz 10 separated from the Salyut and returned to earth.

Had technical difficulties prevented an attempt to move cosmonauts into the laboratory? United States space officials thought that might be the case. "I can only say it appears as if the Soviets failed in their prime mission on this flight," one official remarked. "Any flight that doesn't get the most out of time in space must be suggestive of partial failure."

The Americans wondered why the cosmonauts had not used Soyuz 10's powerful engines to move the combined craft into a higher orbit to prolong the life of the Salyut. The laboratory's low orbit exposed it to the friction of the extreme outer fringes of the atmosphere. Within a few weeks the Salyut would be dragged down into the atmosphere where it would burn up.

Russian officials professed satisfaction with the results of the Soyuz 10 mission. They pointed out that a manned craft and an unmanned ship controlled from the ground had locked in space. Moreover, it was more difficult to dock the Soyuz, a relatively small spaceship, with a large craft like the Salyut than to link two vehicles of equal size. To accomplish the successful linkup, the cosmonauts had used improved systems for search, rendezvous, and docking.

Boris Yegorov, the physician-cosmonaut, observed that the reactions of the Soyuz 10 crew during the intricate docking maneuvers would help in the planning of the future space missions. "Medical men and engineers are looking for and finding the most rational combination of men and automatic equipment to perform such a complex maneuver in orbit," he said.

In a postflight press conference, the Soyuz 10 commander, Vladimir Shatalov, told reporters: "We are still working toward the creation of an orbital space station. The past decade has seen us

move step by step toward the solution of the problem. This flight was one more step."

Shatalov's crewmen, Alexei Yeliseyev and Nikolai Rukavishnikov, also expressed satisfaction with the Soyuz 10 mission. And Rukavishnikov told newsmen: "We are alive, healthy, and in one piece," a remark that all safely returned spacemen could appreciate.

While cosmonauts, space officials, and Western observers evaluated the flight of Soyuz 10, the Salyut continued to travel around the earth. According to Tass, controllers were carrying on a "lively dialogue" with the orbiting laboratory. Tass also hinted that other manned spaceships might join up with the Salyut.

Early in June two members of the Kettering schoolboy tracking team picked up a radio signal from the Salyut. Because the craft had been silent for five weeks, the boys and their teacher surmised that the Russians were getting ready to launch another craft to join the laboratory in space. The boys continued to monitor their radio and on June 6 they heard what they identified as a signal from a three-man spaceship. One of the amateur trackers explained: "A good three-man satellite signal makes a kind of purring noise, followed by fifteen bleeps. The fourth bleep is someone's heartbeat, the eighth identifies the seat the cosmonaut is sitting in, and when we put a name to him we can tell when they move from their seats or go to sleep." He added: "Occasionally, we even hear voice casts from the crew to their ground control."

Using information supplied by the Kettering trackers, British newspapers printed the story of the launching a half hour before the Soviet Union officially announced that a three-man Soyuz spacecraft had gone into orbit to attempt another linkup with the Salyut. According to the announcement, Soyuz 11 would continue scientific and technical studies in a "joint flight" with the orbiting Salyut. The three Soyuz crewmen were described as "comfortable," and all of the spacecraft's systems were functioning normally.

Soyuz 11's commander, Georgi Dobrovolsky, was a former fighter pilot. "I love any kind of flying," he said during an interview before the Soyuz 11 launching. "Whether it is flying an airplane,

Models of the Soyuz 11 spacecraft docking with the Salyut station. Top photo shows the two craft a moment before the docking; lower photo shows the two docked and linked together.

Crew of the Soyuz 11 are shown here in a training craft. From left: Georgi Dobrovolsky (reclining), Viktor Patsayev, and Vladislav Volkov.

descending on a parachute, performing on a trampoline, or jumping from a parachute-training tower.''

As a teen-ager, however, Dobrovolsky wanted to attend a merchant marine academy. When he failed to gain admission, he entered a school that trained boys for the Soviet Air Force. He was later accepted at a four-year flying school. For the forty-three-year-old cosmonaut, it was a first trip into space.

Viktor Patsayev, Soyuz 11's test engineer, was another space rookie. He was thirty-seven years old and had been a design engineer for precision instruments before becoming a cosmonaut in 1968. Since then he had specialized in work on orbital stations.

Vladislav Volkov, the thirty-five-year-old flight engineer, was the only veteran on the Soyuz 11 crew. The cosmonaut had served as a flight engineer during the Soyuz 7 mission in 1969.

The first message from the Salyut-bound Soyuz 11 was a cheery: "On board everything in order, feeling normal." Later the crew reported that they had successfully fired the Soyuz's engines to change its orbit. Their new flight path, ranging between 115 and 135 miles above the earth, would bring them closer to the Salyut.

After twenty-four hours of flight, Soyuz 11 was within 4 miles of its target. Complex automatic systems guided the two ships until they were 350 feet apart. Then Cosmonaut Dobrovolsky took over the Soyuz controls for the linkup. When he finished a series of delicate maneuvers, the Soyuz and the Salyut were docked nose to nose. The combined vehicle was 65 feet long and approximately 13 feet in diameter. It weighed 25 tons.

This time the cosmonauts did what the Soyuz 10 crew had failed to do. They entered the Salyut. Viktor Patsayev was the first to crawl through the tunnel connecting the two craft. Flight Engineer Vladislav Volkov and Mission Commander Dobrovolsky followed, thus completing the first direct ship-to-ship transfer in the Soviet manned space program.

From the tunnel, the cosmonauts entered a small transfer compartment housing astronomical equipment and other instruments. A hatch led into the Salyut's main working compartment. This was a large room equipped with comfortable chairs for the cosmonauts. In all, the Salyut contained about 3,500 cubic feet of living and working area, approximately the space of a 40-foot house trailer. An impressed Cosmonaut Dobrovolsky told ground controllers: "This place is tremendous. There seems to be no end to it." The Salyut terminated in a service module containing fuel tanks and propulsion equipment.

From the Salyut, Dobrovolsky reported that the crew was feeling well and anxious to begin work. During their stay in the orbiting laboratory the cosmonauts were going to check out its equipment, test its navigational instruments, make astronomical observations, and study the earth's geography and atmosphere. They were also going to observe their own reactions to prolonged space travel. However, Soviet officials declined to reveal how long the three would remain in the Salyut.

When the cosmonauts entered the Salyut, its orbit ranged

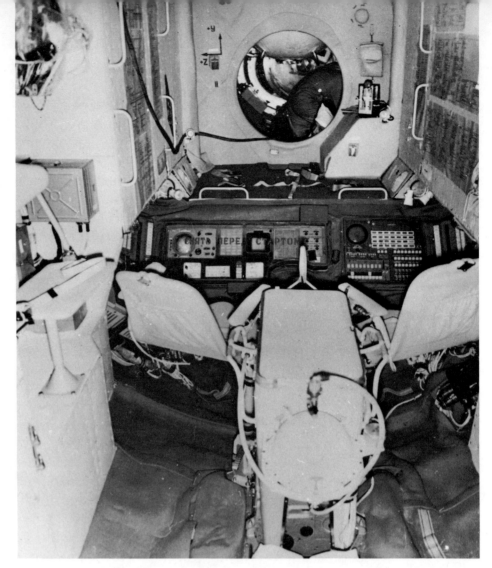

Working compartment of the main section of Salyut. At center is control panel and the chairs of the crew members. Behind panel is entrance to the tunnel connecting the Salyut with the Soyuz 11 spacecraft.

from 132 to 155 miles above the earth. Twenty-four hours later atmospheric drag had pulled it down to an orbit of 130 to 151 miles. The cosmonauts fired the Salyut's engines to raise the craft and the docked Soyuz to a more long-lasting 148- to 165-mile orbit. During the maneuver Dobrovolsky reported: "I see the fire of the mid-correction engines through the porthole. There is a bright flash, a very bright flash, with a very large number of white particles, like a snow blizzard. The particles are passing us in a dense veil in front of the porthole. We have five portholes in front of us. Visibility is good. It is a pleasure to see the earth."

The cosmonaut also said that he saw the flag on the Salyut's aerial fluttering as the ship moved. This was the first mention of the fact that the orbiting laboratory was flying a Soviet flag.

Meanwhile, Soviet scientists on the earth were referring to the Salyut as a cosmodom (space house) and to future space laboratories as cosmograds (space cities), two new words in the growing vocabulary of space terms.

During their third day on board the Salyut, the cosmonauts raised its orbit another 11 miles, an indication that the Soviets wanted to keep their space laboratory aloft for a long time. There was also evidence that the cosmonauts might be staying in space for many days. On Soviet TV they appeared in elastic exercise suits, which they called "penguin suits" because of the way cosmonauts waddled in them when they walked during practice sessions on earth.

Designed to make the wearer use his muscles in the weightlessness of space, the suits resembled tight-fitting overalls. They were constructed of several layers of rubber material that exerted muscle-toning pressure on the cosmonauts' bodies. If a cosmonaut were to relax, the pull of his suit would draw his knees up to his chin and bring his arms together across his chest. The suits also provided tension for the spine and neck.

"We feel much better with the suit on than without it," Commander Dobrovolsky told ground controllers. "Please tell the designers that we are very pleased with it."

In addition to making the cosmonauts more comfortable while in orbit, space officials hoped the suits, combined with a regular exercise program, would ease their readaptation to gravity when they returned to earth. The Soyuz 9 cosmonauts had taken more than a week to recover from their almost eighteen days in orbit. If the penguin suit worked, the Soyuz 11 crew would experience no such problems.

It took the cosmonauts many hours to complete the move into the Salyut. When they finished, they shut down Soyuz 11's man-operated equipment. Their new home contained everything they would need for a long stay in space. The orbiting laboratory's standard of comfort was described as "high." It had heaters for water and food, refrigerators, and even a vacuum cleaner. There was also a library stocked with the cosmonauts' favorite books.

Once they had moved into the Salyut, the cosmonauts settled into a routine of work, exercise, and rest. The effects of weightlessness on their bodies was to be one of their most important studies. The spacemen took periodic blood samples for later analysis on earth. They checked their respiration and pulse rates and measured the calcium content of their bones with a device called a calcimeter. Bones lose small amounts of calcium during weight-lessness and they wanted to obtain a record of the loss.

From their orbiting laboratory the cosmonauts radioed regular reports on areas of cloud cover and other weather phenomena that they observed from space. They also photographed the stars, something that could be done better in space than on earth because of the distorting effects of the earth's atmosphere.

Cosmonaut Patsayev had a special assignment. He was the first space gardener. The Salyut's fluorescent-lit garden contained cabbages and onions in a special nutrient solution. Patsayev watered the garden at the end of each workday.

On June 19, their thirteenth day in space, the cosmonauts took time out from their regular schedule to hold a birthday party. It was Viktor Patsayev's thirty-eighth birthday and the party was a surprise. "While I was busy . . . they brought the dinner table into the working compartment and managed to set it," Patsayev told ground controllers. "Vladislav Volkov presented me with an onion and Georgi Dobrovolsky with a lemon. They had brought their presents from earth and had kept silent about them, wanting to surprise me. I especially enjoyed the onion."

His fellow cosmonauts toasted Patsayev with prune juice. The party fare also included tubes of cottage cheese, juices and pastes, cans of veal, sugared fruit, nuts and prunes.

Soyuz 9's record of 17 days 16 hours 59 minutes in space was broken on June 24. In spite of their many days in orbit, the Soyuz 11 cosmonauts seemed to be in good health. As the days passed, however, they began to feel tired. And they reported that they might have gained weight. "We have no scales; they would be useless anyway," Flight Commander Dobrovolsky told ground controllers. "But we think we haven't lost weight and maybe gained some. We'll see when we're back home."

In their orbiting laboratory the cosmonauts enjoyed a more varied diet than previous Soviet space travelers. The Salyut's food lockers and refrigerators contained beefsteak and other solid foods to supplement the pastes and liquids that had to be eaten from tubes. Although they ate with good appetites, the cosmonauts admitted that they missed home cooking.

When would they be returning to the earth? Soviet space officials remained silent on that subject, but many Russians thought the flight might last as long as a month. They enjoyed watching the daily TV programs from the Salyut when the cheerful cosmonauts could be seen at work, proudly displaying the Salyut's equipment and demonstrating the effects of weightlessness.

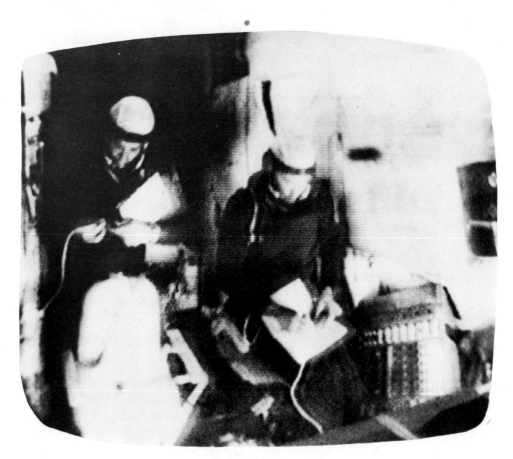

Cosmonauts Dobrovolsky (left) and Volkov in the working compartment of Salyut.

Orders to leave the Salyut reached the cosmonauts on June 29. They began at once to move their logs, records, and experiments back to the Soyuz and to shut down the Salyut's equipment. Then they reactivated and checked the Soyuz's systems.

Shortly before 9:30 P.M., Moscow time, on June 29, Soyuz 11 drew away from the Salyut. From their seats in the Soyuz spacecraft the cosmonauts reported that the unlinking operation had gone smoothly and the Soyuz's equipment was operating well after the long shutdown. "Everything aboard is in order," Commander Dobrovolsky radioed Ground Control. "We feel excellent and are ready for landing."

Flight Engineer Volkov took one last look at the Salyut, which was to remain in orbit. "I see the station," he radioed. "It sparkles in the sun."

Before Soyuz 11 left orbit, one of the ground controllers sent a message to the cosmonauts. "Goodbye, Amber [Soyuz 11's call sign]," he radioed. "We'll soon meet you on your native earth."

"Thank you," Dobrovolsky replied. "Until we see you again."

Soyuz 11 was high over Africa when the always hazardous landing process began. The ship's braking rockets fired and the craft slowed. Its rear and forward compartments separated from the command cabin holding the cosmonauts, and the command cabin started earthward on a carefully planned trajectory that would bring it back to the landing zone in Kazakhstan. The cosmonauts had been in space for 23 days 17 hours 40 minutes. They had traveled some 10,000,000 miles.

As Soyuz 11 fell toward the earth, heat generated by its passage through the thickening atmosphere cut off radio communication with ground controllers. This was something that took place every time a spacecraft returned to earth. It lasted for approximately twelve minutes and was no cause for alarm. There was cause for alarm, however, when the twelve minutes passed and Soyuz 11 remained silent.

Meanwhile, the craft's descent continued. Its landing was automatically controlled. The news agency, Tass, explained what happened. "After aerodynamic braking in the atmosphere, the parachute system was put into action and, before landing, the soft-landing engines were fired. The flight of the descending apparatus ended in a smooth landing."

Within seconds of the landing, a recovery helicopter had touched down near the heat-scarred, and still silent, Soyuz 11. The recovery crew rushed to the spacecraft and opened its hatch. Inside they found the cosmonauts strapped to their seats. All three were dead.

What had happened to bring what had appeared to be a very successful mission to such an unfortunate ending? While Soviet officials launched an investigation, Western space experts suggested that the disaster could have been caused by a failure in Soyuz 11's oxygen supply during, or soon after, the firing of its braking rockets. The cosmonauts were reported to have died with no signs of a struggle and with serene expressions on their faces, which would be the case if the cause of death were hypoxia, or lack of oxygen.

The spacecraft's oxygen lines may have broken, or oxygen may have leaked out of the capsule into the vacuum of space. In either event, the cosmonauts would have begun to feel giddy or drowsy, and their fingernails, lips, and skin would have developed a bluish hue. Death would have come quickly — within minutes — before the cosmonauts realized that anything was amiss.

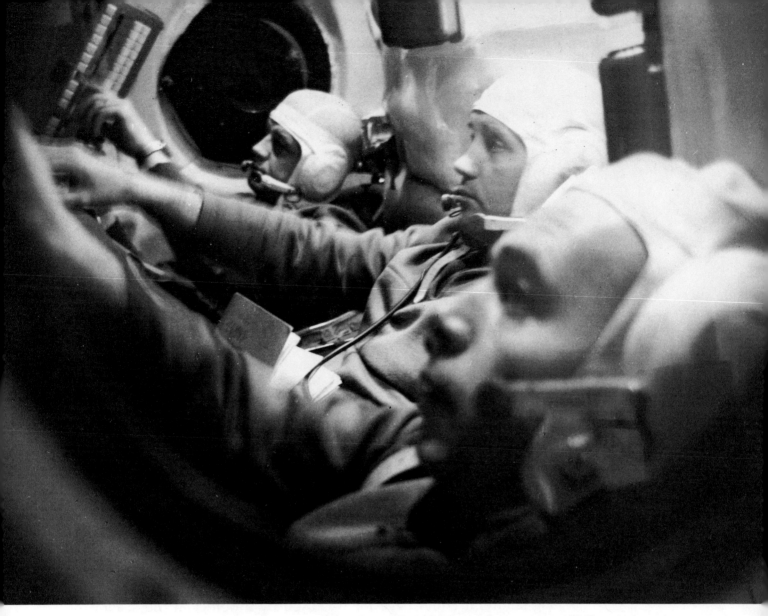

The Soyuz 11 crew in the cabin of the ship. From left: Cosmonauts Volkov, Dobrovolsky, and Patsayev.

There were other possible explanations for the tragic end of the Soyuz 11 mission. Noxious fumes from a small fire or overheated equipment could have entered the cosmonauts' cabin. The spacecraft's heat shield may have failed during reentry into the earth's atmosphere. Or the cosmonauts may have been so weakened by their long period of weightlessness that they could not withstand the stresses of reentry.

Whatever the emergency that occurred aboard Soyuz 11, the cosmonauts had faced it without the protection of pressure suits. On most Soyuz missions cosmonauts did not wear them.

News of the cosmonauts' deaths shocked the Russian people. Grieving men, women, and children gathered to discuss the space tragedy. Many wept openly. Soviet leaders praised the accomplishments of the Soyuz 11 mission and sent messages of condolence to the cosmonauts' families.

Thousands of Soviet citizens traveled to Moscow's House of the Soviet Army where the bodies of Cosmonauts Georgi Dobrovolsky, Vladislav Volkov, and Viktor Patsayev lay in state. Their fellow cosmonauts in dark suits and airmen in light blue uniforms formed a guard of honor around the three flower-covered biers. Government officials joined the honor guard as did American Astronaut Thomas Stafford, who represented President Richard Nixon.

On July 2, a day of national mourning in the Soviet Union, the fallen cosmonauts received a hero's funeral in Red Square. They were buried in the Kremlin wall, the resting place of Cosmonauts Yuri Gagarin and Vladimir Komarov and Chief Designer Sergei Korolev.

After nearly two weeks of study, the special committee investigating the Soyuz 11 deaths issued its report. The cosmonauts had been killed when their spaceship suddenly lost pressurization. This apparently occurred some thirty minutes before the landing when Soyuz 11 began its reentry into the earth's atmosphere. The sudden pressure drop resulted from a failure of the ship's hatch to seal properly when the cosmonauts closed off their landing, or command, module prior to jettisoning the Soyuz's orbital module.

Although the report did not pinpoint the reason for the sealing failure, it could have been caused by a defect in the sealing material, or in the way it was installed around the hatch. Or the cosmonauts may have failed to close the hatch completely. In the sudden vacuum created in Soyuz 11 by the leak, the cosmonauts' blood "boiled" and they died within seconds.

Despite the tragic ending of the first attempt to transfer cosmonauts from a Soyuz spacecraft to a Salyut orbiting laboratory, Soviet oficials announced that the Salyut program would continue.

The remaining cosmonauts also expressed their determination to continue the exploration of space. In a joint letter printed in the Communist party paper *Pravda* they said: "We know that our road is a difficult and thorny one, but we never doubted the correctness of our choice and were always ready for any difficult flight.

"We express firm confidence that what happened cannot stop the further development and perfection of space engineering and man's striving for space, striving for knowledge of the mysteries of the universe."

In another *Pravda* article, space scientist Petrov praised the efforts of the pioneering Soyuz 11 crew and predicted: "One can say with confidence that the 1970's will become an epoch in the development and wide use of long-term manned orbiting stations with crews that change, which will make it possible to go from occasional experiments in space to a regular vigil by scientists and experts in space laboratories."

Sometime during the 1970's, perhaps as early as 1973, the United States plans to launch its first orbiting space platform. Called Skylab, the American program has many objectives in common with the Soviet Salyut, including laying the groundwork for a permanent, manned space station.

Similarities between the two programs and other space efforts of the United States and the Soviet Union have prompted scientists in both countries to suggest that they cooperate in the exploration of space. Such cooperation would reduce both the danger and the high monetary cost of space activity.

There has already been some limited cooperation between the United States and the Soviet Union. Both have signed a United Nations treaty dealing with care of space crewmen who land in foreign countries. They have also agreed to exchange data gathered by weather satellites. Samples of moon rock and soil collected by American astronauts have been presented to Soviet scientists. In return, American scientists have received samples of rock and soil returned to earth by Luna 16.

Soviet and American scientists meet regularly at international conferences where information acquired during space flights is exchanged. Several of the cosmonauts have visited the United States and American astronauts have visited the Soviet Union.

Within a few years some of the equipment and procedures used on Soviet and American spacecraft may be standardized, allowing cosmonauts and astronauts to rescue one another in space. According to some scientists, in the future as many as one hundred men may be in space at the same time — in space stations, in space shuttles ferrying people to and from the stations, in orbit around the moon, or on the moon. Sooner or later, one of the spacecraft will be in trouble and a ship belonging to another country might be the only one in a position to speed to the rescue. However, it would be able to give effective help only if the two ships were using the same radio frequency and their maneuvering and

American Astronauts Buzz Aldrin and Neil Armstrong (second from left) welcome Soviet Cosmonauts Nikolayev and Sevastyanov at Washington National Airport in October, 1970, where they began a ten-day tour of the United States. (NASA photo)

docking procedures, docking mechanisms, pressure-suit connections, and cabin atmospheres were similar.

When the Soviet Union and the United States have adopted standardized equipment and procedures, astronauts could move from a disabled Skylab-bound ferry ship to a Soyuz. Likewise, the Americans could remove cosmonauts from a malfunctioning Russian craft. It would also be possible for American and Russian craft to join up in space to form an international space station. Scientists from the two countries could then carry out studies together in space as they have already done to some extent in Antarctica.

Cosmonauts and astronauts look favorably upon the idea of

IN MEMORY OF

YURI GAGARIN

FIRST MAN IN SPACE, APRIL 12, 1961

FROM THE ASTRONAUTS OF THE
UNITED STATES OF AMERICA.

JOHN H. GLENN, Jr.
for
MERCURY ASTRONAUTS

JAMES A. McDIVITT
for
GEMINI ASTRONAUTS

NEIL ARMSTRONG
for
APOLLO ASTRONAUTS

A plaque presented to the USSR in 1971 by the National Aeronautics and Space Administration in memory of Soviet Cosmonaut Yuri Gagarin, who lost his life in a training accident in 1968. (NASA photo)

working together in space. During a press conference when he was visiting the United States in 1969, Cosmonaut Georgi Beregovoi said about such cooperation: "We are going parallel, but different, ways now, but in principle such a possibility exists — maybe as soon as we learn English."

And Apollo 15 Astronaut David Scott told reporters at another press conference: "I know six of the cosmonauts personally and they are great people. I would fly with them any day and hope to be able to sometime."

In addition to orbiting the earth in spaceships and space stations, perhaps with astronauts as crewmates, the Soviet Union's cosmonauts expect to travel to more distant points in space. Cosmonaut Konstantin Feoktistov has said that the Soviet Union has plans to fly men to the vicinity of Mars, Venus, and Mercury, the three nearest planets. They will fly past the planets or orbit them since men can probably not survive on Venus or Mercury and a Mars landing would be very difficult.

Although the Soviet Union has ruled out any immediate landing on the moon, cosmonauts may go there as well, especially if the Russians succeed in developing the powerful booster that would be needed. On the moon the cosmonauts will be able to supplement the work already done by the astronauts and the unmanned Lunas and Lunokhods.

Wherever they go as they extend their exploration of space, the cosmonauts will be continuing the work that began in the Soviet Union long before the first rocket left a launching pad. They will have the valuable information gathered by the cosmonauts who orbited the earth in Vostok, Voskhod, and Soyuz spaceships to help them as they remain aloft for longer periods and travel farther from the earth. If the Soviet government continues to support their efforts, as it has in the past, that country, and the world, can look forward to a greater understanding of space and the ways it can be used to benefit the inhabitants of the earth.

INDEX

Acceleration forces, 14, 16, 18, 54
Agena rocket, 111
Air-lock chamber, 101, 104, 106
Air system of Soviet spacecraft, 101, 129
Airplanes, early Russian, 22-25, 30
Aldrin, Edwin, 132, 153
Alexander II, Czar, 26
Animal space flights, 20, 35, 39-40, 53, 58-59, 60, 162
Apogee, 62
Apollo, Project, 79-80, 86, 111, 112, 118, 132
    cabin size, 114
    capsule fire, 111
    first lunar orbit, 124
    first moon landing, 132
Apollo 7, 118
Apollo 8, 124, 132
Apollo 9, 132
Apollo 10, 132
Apollo 11, 132, 141, 153-154, 155
Apollo 12, 155
Armstrong, Neil, 132, 141, 153
"Astronaut" versus "cosmonaut," terminology, 10
Automatic guidance system, 15, 107
Aviation, Russian, history of, 22-25, 30

Baikonur cosmodrome, 10. *See also* Tyuratam
Balance, sense of, during weightlessness, 66, 97
Balloon flight, 22, 26
Belyayev, Pavel Ivanovich, 102
    biographical data, 102
    training of, 102-103
    Voskhod 2 flight of, 103-110

Bends, the, 101
Beregovoi, Georgi T., 118, 124, 131, 181
    biographical data, 118-119
    Soyuz 3 flight of, 118, 119-122, 123, 131
Borman, Frank, 143
Brezhnev, Leonid I., 132
Bykovsky, Valery Fyodorovich, 84
    biographical data, 85
    Vostok 5 flight of, 84-91, 143

Cape Kennedy, Fla., 20, 125, 138
Carpenter, M. Scott, 71, 79
Centrifuge training machine, 54
Chaffee, Roger, 111
Chamber of Silence, 54-56, 73
Chief Designers, Soviet, 45-48, 112
Collins, Michael, 132, 153
Color vision, in space, 142
Communications relay system, Soyuz 8 test, 137, 138
Communications satellites, 86, 147, 162
Congreve, William, 25
Cooper, Gordon, 85
Cosmodom, 173
Cosmodromes, 10, 48-50
Cosmograd, 173
Cosmonauts:
    choice of term, 10
    factors in selection of, 51, 86
    fatalities, 116, 118, 176-178
    first, 7, 13, 21, 57
    medical testing of, 10, 52, 54
    psychological testing of, 10, 52, 55-56, 60
    recruitment of, 51-52, 86

residence of, 48
secrecy about, 51
training of, 10, 52-57, 81, 86-87,
143
women, 85-87, 88
Cosmos satellites, 71, 75, 112, 162
Crash landing, 147

Deaths. *See* Fatalities
Deceleration forces, 16, 18, 68, 82-84,
100
DeGaulle, Charles, 141
Descent of Soviet spaceships, 16, 58.
See also Landing system; Reentry
Dirigibles, 26, 29-30
Discoverer satellite, 21
Dobrovolsky, Georgi, 169
biographical data, 169-170
death of, 176-178
in Soyuz II flight, 169, 171-176
Docking, space, 79, 91, 111, 121, 123,
124, 137, 138
first (Gemini 8 with Agena), 111
first Soviet, Soyuz 4 with 5, 128-
129, 132, 136
Soyuz 10 with Salyut, 166-167
Soyuz II with Salyut, 171
Dogs, space, 39-40, 53, 58, 59, 60
Dornberger, Walter, 33, 34
Drinking, during space flight, 65, 89
Dushkin, L. S., 33

Earth:
early cosmonaut descriptions of,
15, 62, 63-64, 65
escape velocity, 40
orbital velocity, 40
Eating, during space flight, 11, 15, 64-
65, 88. *See also* Food
Eisenhower, Dwight D., 21, 35
Ejection system, on Vostoks, 16, 116
Electronic-beam welding, 137
Escape velocity, earth gravitational, 40
EVA (extravehicular activity), 111. *See
also* Space walks
Exercise, during space flight, 68, 142,
146, 173
Explorer 1, 20-21, 40

Extravehicular activity. *See* EVA; Space
walks

Fatalities, 118
Apollo fire, 111
Soviet, in flight, 116, 176-178
Feoktistov, Konstantin P., 92, 103, 182
biographical data, 92-93
training of, 93-94
in Voskhod 1 flight, 96-100
Filipchenko, Anatoly, 134, 137, 146
Fire, capsule, 101
Apollo accident, 111
Food, during space flight, 11, 15, 64-
65, 81, 88, 99, 136, 174
Fuels, rocket, 26, 31, 32, 33
Fyodorov, Y. S., 23

g-forces, 14, 16, 18, 68, 82, 96-97
readaptation to, 145-146, 173
training program, 54
Gagarin, Yuri Alexeyevich, 7-18, 20,
51, 52, 57, 60, 113, 116, 118, 178
biographical data, 7-9
death of, 118
space mission of, 7, 10-16, 21, 60,
68
training of, 10, 52-57
mentioned, 22, 47, 61, 63, 69, 78,
86, 87, 96, 119, 126
Gemini 8, 111
Gemini 3, 111
Gemini 4, 111
Gemini 6, 111, 135
Gemini 7, 111, 135, 142, 143
Gemini 8, 111
German V-2 rocket, 33-35, 47
Geshvend, Fydor R., 26
Glenn, John H., Jr., 71, 98
Glushko, V. P., 33
Goddard, Robert H., 31
Gorbatko, Viktor, 135
Grissom, Virgil, 111
Ground trace, 50
Group flight (*see also* Docking; Ren-
dezvous):
Soyuzes 6 to 8, 135-137, 138
Vostoks 3 and 4, 78-79, 84, 91
Vostoks 5 and 6, 88-89, 91

Heat shield, reentry, 68-69
Heavier-than-air craft, history of, 22-
23, 26, 30
Helicopter prototypes, 22, 23

ICIC (Interdepartmental Commission
on Interplanetary Communications),
35, 45
IGY (International Geophysical Year),
36, 37
Ilyushin, Sergei, 46
International space cooperation, 179-
181
"Interplanetary communications," So-
viet terminology, 32
Iron Maiden, 54
Isolation training, 54-56, 73

Jet propulsion, 25, 26, 47
Jodrell Bank Observatory, 42, 79
Jupiter C rocket, 40

Kapustin Yar cosmodrome, 48
Katyushka rocket, 33
Keldysh, Mstislav V., 163
Kennedy, John F., 20
Khrunov, Yevgeny, 124
    biographical data, 126-128
    in Soyuz 5 flight, 124, 126, 129
    space-walk transfer to Soyuz 4,
        129-131
Khrushchev, Nikita, 9-10, 17, 63, 65,
69, 73, 116
Kibalchich, Nicholas, 26
Kinetic theory of gases, 28-29
Komarov, Vladimir Mikhailovich, 92,
103, 137, 178
    biographical data, 92
    death of, 115-116, 118
    training of, 92, 102
    Soyuz 1 flight of, 112-113, 115-
        116
    in Voskhod 1 flight, 92, 96-100
Konstantinov, Konstantin, 26
Konstantovitch, Nikolai, 53
Korolev, Sergei Pavlovich, 45-48, 50-
51, 58, 112, 178
    booster rockets of, 45, 50-51, 94,
        96

and Sputnik, 45, 47, 50
and Voskhod program, 45, 48, 94,
    96, 99, 100, 101
and Vostok program, 45, 48, 50-
    51, 56-57, 60, 71, 87, 88
Kosygin, Alexei N., 116, 141
Kubasov, Valery N., 134
    biographical data, 134
    in Soyuz 6 flight, 134, 135, 136-
        137

Laika (space dog), 39-40
Landing systems, 116, 131
    separate parachutes for craft and
        pilot, 16, 53, 68, 69, 84
    soft landing on land, 16, 100, 116
    soft versus crash, 147
    Soyuz 1 failure, 115-116
    U.S., on water, 100, 116
Launching:
    g-force during, 14, 16, 18, 54, 96-
        97
    television broadcasts of, 125
Launching sites, Russian, 10, 48-50
Leonardo da Vinci, 23
Leonov, Alexei A., 101, 128, 131
    biographical data, 102
    space walk of, 104-106, 110
    training of, 102, 103
    Voskhod 2 flight of, 103-110
Life line, for space walk, 105
Life-support unit, for space walk, 104,
105
Lighter-than-air craft, 29-30
Lodyghin, Alexander, 23
Lomonosov, Mikhail, 22
Lovell, Sir Bernard, 20, 79
Lovell, James A., 143
Luna spacecraft, 9, 21, 40-44, 45, 147-
151, 153-159
    launch site, 49
    rocket, 50
    weight of various, 40, 153, 154
Luna 1, 40-42, 44, 147
Luna 2 (first landing), 42-43, 147
Luna 3 (orbital), 43-44, 147
Lunas 4-8 (failures), 147-149
Luna 9 (soft landing), 149, 152

Luna 10 (moon satellite), 149-150
Luna 11, 150
Luna 12, 150
Luna 13, 151
Luna 14, 153
Luna 15, 153-154
Luna 16 (soil sample returned), 154-155, 159, 179
Luna 17 (with mooncar), 155-159
Luna 20, 159
Lunar Orbiter spacecraft, 152
Lunokhod, 156-159

Manned space flight, 51, 57, 60
    first, 7, 13-16, 21, 60
    first American, 20
    first multimanned mission, 92-100
    future outlook, 178-182
    to moon, 79-80, 110, 111-112, 124, 132, 152, 182
    pilots, selection factors, 51, 86
    Soviet, see Soyuz; Voskhod; Vostok
    space stations a Soviet priority, 132, 143, 146, 163
    time records, 142-143, 174-176
    training for, 52-57
    U.S., see Apollo; Gemini; Mercury
    versus unmanned, 155
Manual control
    in docking, 128, 166, 171
    Soyuz 3, 120, 121
    Voskhod 2, 107-108
    Vostok 2, 60, 61, 62-63, 66
Mariner spacecraft, 162
Mars, 51, 147, 162, 182
Mars spacecraft, 162
Medical tests of cosmonauts. See Physical tests
Mendeléyev, Dmitri, 22
Mercury (planet), 182
Mercury, Project, 20, 51, 53, 71
Meshchersky, Ivan, 26
Meteorological rockets, 36. See also Weather satellites
Mikhailov, Onisim, 25
Military rocketry, 33-34, 35, 48
Military satellites, 147, 162

Molniya communications satellites, 137, 162, 167
Moon:
    distance from earth, 157
    first photos of far side, 43-44
    length of day on, 157
Moon exploration, 9, 21, 40-44, 118, 147-159
    first artificial satellite of moon (Luna 10), 149-150
    first manned landing (Apollo 11), 132, 153-154
    first manned orbital mission (Apollo 8), 124, 132
    first unmanned landing (Luna 2), 42
    first unmanned soft landing and instrument package (Luna 9), 149, 152
    hard versus soft landing, 147, 152
    manned versus unmanned, 155
    Soviet Luna program, see Luna
    speculations about Soviet intent, 79, 110, 111-112, 132, 163, 182
    of surface, 149-151, 152, 154-155, 157-159
    U.S. program, 79, 110, 111, 112, 124, 132, 151-152 (see also Apollo; Lunar Orbiter; Ranger; Surveyor)
    Zond spacecraft, 159
Moon Rover, 156
Mozhaisky, Alexander, 22-23
Multistage rockets, 30-31
    first unmanned orbital mission (Luna 3), 43-44

National Aeronautics and Space Administration (NASA), 20, 45, 79, 86, 111, 143
Navigational satellites, 21
Nehru, Jawaharlal, 20
Neptune (cosmonaut newspaper), 102
Nesmeyanov, A. N., 18, 35
Nikolayev, Andrian G., 61, 71, 85, 131, 138-139
    biographical data, 71, 91, 139
    effect of prolonged weightlessness on, 145-146

in Soyuz 9 flight, 138-143, 145
training of, 71-73, 78, 81
Vostok 3 flight of, 73-84, 89, 139, 145
Nitrogen, in capsule air system, 101, 129
Nixon, Richard M., 178

Oberth, Hermann, 31
OR-1 rocket (Tsander), 32
OR-2 rocket (Tsander), 33
Orbit, apogee and perigee of, 62
Orbital velocity, earth, 40
ORM-52 rocket (Glushko), 33
Oxygen:
in capsule air system, 101
lack of (hypoxia), 176
supply during space walk, 105

Parachutes, use for cosmonauts' descent, 16, 53, 68, 69, 84, 116
Patsayev, Viktor, 170
biographical data, 170-171
death of, 176-178
in Soyuz 11 flight, 170, 171, 174
"Penguin suit," 173
Perigee, 62
Perquet, Guido von, 31
Peter I, Czar, 25
Physical tests of cosmonauts, 10, 52, 54
in-flight monitoring, 11, 62, 63, 80, 81-82, 85, 134, 136, 138, 141-142, 173-174
by physician aboard, 96, 97
postflight, 17, 84, 145
of prolonged weightlessness, 141-142, 145, 173-174
Physician-cosmonaut, 92, 93, 97, 167
Pioneer satellite, 21
Planetary exploration, 51, 147, 155, 159-162, 182
Plesetsk, launch site near, 50
Podgorny, Nikolai, 116
Popovich, Pavel, 76
biographical data, 76
space flight training of, 78, 81
Vostok 4 flight of, 76-84
Pressure suit. See Space suit

Psychological tests of cosmonauts, 10, 52, 55-56, 60
Pyrotechnics, 25

Radiation studies, 21, 40, 162
Ranger spacecraft, 151-152
Reaction motion, 30
Record, time spent in space, 142-143, 174-176
Recovery of Soviet spaceships, 16, 58
Redstone rocket, 20
Reentry, 15-16, 31, 68-69, 82-84, 107-108
automatic guidance, 15, 107
communications blackout, 176
danger of, 59-60, 115-116
g-force during, 16, 18, 68, 82, 84
by manual control, Voskhod 2, 107-108
Soyuz 11 tragedy, 176-178
Rendezvous in space, 79, 111 (see also Docking; Group flights)
Gemini 6 with 7, 111
Soyuz 3 with 2, 120-122
Research satellites, 147, 162
Rocket fuels, 26, 31, 32, 33
Rocket planes, 26
Rocket propulsion, 26, 30-31
Rocketry, Russian, 34-44, 50-51, 96
early history, 22, 25-33
military, 35, 47, 48, 147
secrecy of, 35, 45, 48-51
Rukavishnikov, Nikolai, 164, 169
Ryhachev, M. A., 23

Saint Exupéry, Antoine de, 134
Salyut, 163, 166-167, 169, 171-175, 178
date launched, 163
description of, 166-167, 171, 173
docking of Soyuz 10 with, 166-167
docking of Soyuz 11 with, 171, 175
orbit of, 163, 164, 167, 171-172, 173
size of, 166, 171
Soyuz 11 crew in, 171-175
weight of, 163
Satellites, manmade, 147, 162 (see also

Cosmos; Sputnik; Unmanned space-
flight)
   first, 20-21, 36-39
Saturn rocket, 79
Score, Project, 21
Scott, David, 181
Secrecy of Soviet space program, 35,
   45, 48-51, 75, 82, 112, 124, 125, 132
Sedov, Leonid I., 35, 132
Seryogin, Vladimir S., 118
Sevastyanov, Vitaly I., 138
   biographical data, 139-140
   effect of prolonged weightless-
      ness on, 145-146
   in Soyuz 9 flight, 138-143
Shatalov, Vladimir, 124, 135, 163-164
   biographical data, 124
   commander of seven-man group
      flight, 135, 163
   Soyuz 4 flight of, 124-125, 128-
      131, 135
   in Soyuz 8 flight, 135-136, 138
   in Soyuz 10 mission, 163-169
Shepard, Alan B., Jr., 20
Shonin, Gregory S., 133-134, 136-137
Sikorsky, Igor, 23
Simulators, training in, 53-54
Skylab, 179, 180
Sleeping, in space flight, 66-67
Soft landing, 147, 152
Sokovin, Nicholas, 26
Solar cell panels, Soyuz craft, 114
Solar energy batteries, 31, 156, 157
Soyuz program, 112, 123, 124, 159,
   162, 177
   cabin of craft, 114, 142
   chief designer, 112
   delay due to fatal accident, 118
   and docking, 123, 124, 128-129,
      132, 137, 138, 166-167, 171
   landing system, 116, 131
   meaning of term, 112
   preparation for space stations,
      113-114, 124, 129, 132, 143,
      146, 167-169
   rendezvous, 120-122
   three-craft group flight, 135-137
Soyuz 1, 112-116, 118, 124, 162
   date of flight, 112

description of craft, 114
landing accident, 115-116, 118,
   121, 122
number of orbits, 115
orbit of, 112
purpose of flight, 112, 113-114
reentry of, 115
speed of, 112
weight of, 114
Soyuz 2, 119-122, 123
   date of flight, 120
   orbit of, 120
   rendezvous with Soyuz 3, 120-122
Soyuz 3, 118-122, 123, 124, 126
   date of flight, 118
   duration of flight, 122
   landing of, 122, 131
   manual control, 120, 121
   number of orbits, 122
   orbit of, 120
   rendezvous with Soyuz 2, 120-122
Soyuz 4, 124-125, 128-131, 134, 135,
   163, 164
   date of flight, 124
   docking with Soyuz 5, 128-129,
      136
   duration of flight, 131
   landing of, 131
   number of orbits, 131
   orbit of, 125, 128
   space-walk transfer of two cos-
      monauts from Soyuz 5, 129, 132
Soyuz 5, 124, 125-129, 131, 134, 135,
   163
   crew of, 124, 125-128
   date of flight, 124
   docking with Soyuz 4, 128-129,
      136
   number of orbits, 131
   orbit of, 128
   space-walk transfer to Soyuz 4,
      129, 132
Soyuz 6, 132-134, 135, 136-137, 163
   crew of, 133-134
   date of flight, 132
   duration of flight, 137
   in group flight with Soyuz 7 and
      8, 135-137, 138
   number of orbits, 137

orbit of, 132, 134
purposes of mission, 132-133, 136-137
Soyuz 7, 134-135, 136-137, 163, 171
    crew of, 134-135
    date of flight, 134
    duration of flight, 137
    in group flight with Soyuz 6 and 8, 135-137, 138
    number of orbits, 137
    orbit of, 134
    purposes of mission, 135, 136
Soyuz 8, 135-138, 163, 164
    crew of, 135
    date of flight, 135
    duration of flight, 138
    in group flight with Soyuz 6 and 7, 135-137, 138
    number of orbits, 137-138
    orbit of, 136
    purposes of mission, 136, 137
Soyuz 9, 138-146
    cabin description, 142
    crew of, 138-140
    date of flight, 138
    distance traveled, 143
    duration of flight, 143, 173, 174
    number of orbits, 143
    purposes of mission, 140-141
Soyuz 10, 163-169
    crew of, 163-164
    date of flight, 163
    docking with Salyut, 166-167
    orbit of, 164
Soyuz 11, 169-179
    crew of, 169-171
    distance traveled, 176
    docking with Salyut, 171, 175
    duration of mission, 176
    orbit of, 171
    purposes of mission, 169, 171, 173-174
    reentry, and death of crew, 176-178
Space stations, 79, 100, 101, 110, 113-114, 124, 163-181
    docking of Soyuz 4 with 5 hailed as, 129
    first (Salyut), 163, 166-167, 171-175, 178
    Soviet priority, 132, 143, 146, 163, 179
Space suits:
    not used in Soyuz, 177
    not used in Voskhod, 96
    for space walk, 104, 106
    in Vostok program, 11
Space travel:
    early predictions of, 29, 30, 31, 32, 35
    early societies for, 32
Space walks, 111
    first (Leonov on Voskhod 2), 104-106, 110
    life line, 105
    life-support unit, 104, 105, 129
    pressure suit for, 104, 106
    Soviet air-lock chamber for, 101, 104, 106
    on Soyuz 4 and 5 mission, 129, 132
    White's, Gemini 4, 111
Spacecraft assembly and testing, 138
Spacecraft 1, 58
Spacecraft 2, 58
Spacecraft 3, 59-60
Spacecraft 4, 60
Spacecraft 5, 60
Speed. See Velocity
Sputnik program, 33, 34, 36-40, 45
    launch site, 49
    meaning of term, 36
    rocket, 50
Sputnik 1, 9, 20-21, 36-39, 47
    specifications, 36-37
Sputnik 2, 9, 21, 39-40
    specifications, 21, 39
Sputnik 3, 9, 40
Stafford, Thomas, 178
Surveyer spacecraft, 152

Telstar 2, 86
Tereshkova, Valentina, 86, 131
    biographical data, 86
    married to cosmonaut Nikolayev, 91
    training of, 86-87
    Vostok 6 flight of, 86, 88-91

Thermal chamber, use in training, 56
Thrust:
    early rockets, 32-33
    Vostok and Voskhod, 96
Tikhonrarov, Michael, 33, 35
Titov, Gherman, 48, 57, 60, 71, 81
    biographical data, 60
    Gagarin's backup, 10-11, 49, 57
    training of, 52-57, 58, 60, 73
    Vostok 2 flight of, 60-70, 75, 97
Training of cosmonauts, 10, 52-57, 81, 143
    women cosmonauts, 86-87
Tretesky, I. I., 26
Tsander, Friedrich, 32-33, 47
Tsiolkovsky, Konstantin E., 27-32, 36, 44, 47
Tsiolkovsky formula, 31
Tyuratam cosmodrome, 10-11, 36, 48-49, 58, 138

Unmanned spaceflight, 147-162
    Soviet Cosmos, 71, 75, 112, 162
    Soviet Lunas, 9, 40-44, 147-151, 153-159 (see also Luna)
    Soviet Mars craft, 162
    Soviet Spacecraft 1-5, 58-60
    Soviet Sputniks, 9, 36-40 (see also Sputnik)
    Soviet Veneras, 159-162
    Soviet Zonds, 159, 162
    U.S., 20-21, 40, 111, 151-152, 161, 162
    versus manned, 155
U.S. space program, 20-21, 34, 37-39, 40, 79-80, 82, 85
    first man in orbit, 71
    first satellite, 20-21, 40
    longest manned mission, 142, 143
    Lunar Orbiters, 152
    Mars probes, 162
    military aspects, 35
    moon as goal, 79, 110, 111, 112, 124, 132, 151-152
    Project Apollo, 79-80, 86, 111, 112, 118, 124, 132, 153-154, 155
    Project Gemini, 101, 111
    Project Mercury, 20, 51, 53, 71

    Rangers, 151-152
    selection of astronauts, 51, 86
    Skylab, 179, 180
    Surveyors, 152
    Venus probes, 161

V-2 rocket, 33-35, 47
Van Allen radiation belts, 40
Vanguard, Project, 21, 37-39, 40
Velocity:
    earth orbital, 40
    escape of earth gravity, 40
    of V-2, 33
Venera spacecraft, 159-162
Venus, 51, 147, 159-162, 182
Vibration stand, use in training, 56
Vision, effect of space environment on, 142
Vladimir Komarov, the, 137
Volkov, Vladislav, 134
    biographical data, 134-135
    death of, 176-178
    in Soyuz 7 flight, 134-135
    in Soyuz 11 mission, 171, 174, 175
Volynov, Boris, 124
    biographical data, 125-126
    in Soyuz 5 flight, 124, 125, 128-129, 131
Von Braun, Wernher, 33, 34
Voskhod program, 45, 48, 92
    booster rocket, 94, 96
    Chief Designer, 94, 96, 100-101
    engine thrust, 96
    landing system, 100, 116
    meaning of term, 92
    space suits dispensed with, 96
Voskhod 1, 92-100
    crew of, 92-94
    date of flight, 92
    description of capsule, 94-95
    duration of flight, 99
    landing of, 100
    launching of, 96-97
    main assignment of, 99
    number of orbits, 99
    orbit of, 97
    reentry of, 99-100
    weight of, 95

Voskhod 2, 100-110, 111
    air-lock chamber of, 101, 104, 106
    crew of, 101-102
    date of flight, 103
    landing of, 108-109
    launching of, 104
    manual control, 107-108
    number of orbits, 107
    orbit of, 104, 106
    reentry, 107-108
    space walk, 104-106, 110
    speed of, 105
    weight of, 108
Vostok program, 7, 45, 48, 56-57, 60, 71
    booster rocket of, 50-51, 96
    Chief Designer, 47-48, 50-51
    ejection system of, 16, 116
    engine thrust, 96
    group flights, 78-79, 84, 88-89, 91
    landing system, 16, 68, 69, 84, 116
    launch site, 49
    meaning of term, 7
    use of space suits, 11
Vostok 1, 7, 11-16, 21, 48, 60
    automatic control system of, 15, 59
    count down, 13-14
    date of flight, 7, 20
    duration of flight, 16
    landing, 16
    launching, 14, 49
    orbit of, 7
    reentry, 15-16, 18
    speed of, 14
    weight of, 7
Vostok 2, 60-69, 71
    date of flight, 61
    duration of flight, 69, 75
    landing, 68, 69
    launching, 61-62
    manual control of, 60, 61, 62-63, 66
    number of orbits, 68
    orbit of, 62
    reentry, 68-69
    speed of, 62
Vostok 3, 71, 73-84, 139
    date of launching, 73

distance traveled, 82
    duration of flight, 75, 82
    in group flight with Vostok 4, 78-79, 84
    landing of, 82-84
    launching of, 73
    number of orbits, 82
    orbit of, 73
    purpose of mission, 74-76
    speed of, 73
Vostok 4, 76-84, 92
    date of launching, 76
    distance traveled, 84
    duration of flight, 84
    in group flight with Vostok 3, 78-79, 84
    landing of, 84
    launching of, 76
    number of orbits, 84
    orbit of, 76
    purpose of mission, 76
Vostok 5, 84-86, 88-91, 126
    date of launching, 84
    distance traveled, 89
    duration of flight, 89, 91, 142, 143
    in group flight with Vostok 6, 88-89, 91
    landing of, 89
    number of orbits, 89
    orbit of, 88
    purpose of mission, 85, 91
Vostok 6, 86, 87, 88-91
    date of launching, 86
    duration of flight, 89
    in group flight with Vostok 5, 88-89, 91
    landing of, 89
    number of orbits, 89
    orbit of, 88
    purpose of mission, 91

Weather satellites, 21, 147, 162, 179. *See also* Meteorological rockets
Webb, James E., 20
Weight of spacecraft:
    Explorer 1, 21
    Luna 15, 153
    Luna 16, 154
    Salyut space station, 163

Soyuz 1, 114
Sputnik 1, 21, 36
Sputnik 2, 21, 39
Sputnik 3, 40
V-2 rocket, 33
Venera 4, 160
Voskhod 1, 95
Voskhod 2, 108
Vostok 1, 7
Weightlessness, 14, 15, 62, 70, 80, 81, 97
    and eating, 14, 64-65
    effects of prolonged, 141-142, 145-146, 173-174, 176
    effects on Titov, 66, 70, 81, 97
    effects on vision, 142
    exercise during, 68, 142, 146, 173
    and sense of balance, 66, 97
    and sleeping, 67
    training, 54, 81
    welding during, 133, 136-137
    writing during, 14, 65-66
Welding tests, in space, 133, 136-137
White, Edward, 111

Women cosmonauts, 85-87, 88
World War II, 25, 33-34
Wright brothers, 30
Writing, at zero gravity, 14, 65-66

Yangel, Mikhail K., 112
Yegorov, Boris Borisovich, 93, 103, 167
    biographical data, 93
    training of, 93-94
    in Voskhod 1 flight, 96-100
Yeliseyev, Alexei, 124, 135, 163-164
    biographical data, 126
    in Soyuz 5 flight, 124, 126, 129, 135
    in Soyuz 8 flight, 135-136
    in Soyuz 10 mission, 163-169
    space-walk transfer to Soyuz 4, 129-131

Zasiadko, Alexander, 25
Zero gravity. *See* Weightlessness
Zhukovsky, Nikolai, 23
Zond spacecraft, 159, 162

Colonel Gene Gurney, a U.S. Air Force information specialist with many books to his credit, often teams with his wife, Clare, a former librarian. For Franklin Watts, Inc., they have co-authored such books as *Monticello, Mount Vernon,* and *FDR and Hyde Park.* The Gurneys make their home at Dares Beach, Maryland.